C-5 Galaxy

Written by Richard Lippincott

In Action

Squadron Signal Publications

Cover Art by Don Greer

(Front Cover) A C-5B Galaxy in the "Equipment Excellence" color scheme over the Grand Canyon. Initially seen as a symbol of government excess and poor program management, the C-5 has survived Congressional and media scrutiny to become an indispensable strategic asset, thanks to its unprecedented cargo and range capabilities.

Acknowledgements

Tech. Sgt. Dan Allsup, USAF
Capt. Jeremy Angel, USAFR
Col. Regina Aune, USAF
Tech. Sgt. Andrew Biscoe, USAFR
Keith Boughner
Master Sgt. Rodney Christa, USAFR
Maj. Jennifer Christovich, USAFR
Staff Sgt. Steven Colburn, USAF
Lt. Theresa Conner, USAF
Chuck Corway
Tony D'Anjou
Joe DesRosiers
Senior Airman Andy Dunaway, USAF
Capt. Mike Fox, USAF
Tech. Sgt. Efrain Gonzalez, USAF
Lt. Col. Robert Grudziecki, USAFR
Airman 1st Class Kristi Hare, USAF
Joan Harz
Carl Harz
Sgt. Carl F. Harz, U.S. Army
Col. Thomas R. Hughes, USAF
Nancy Jefferies
Staff Sgt. Suzanne M. Jenkins
Garfield F. Jones
Kevin Keefe
Bill Koster

Kurt Kunze
Mary Lamb
Mike Leister
Karen Lippincott
Airman 1st Class Tiffany Low, USAF
Alan McKown
Maj. Elana T. Milford, USAFR
Airman Brian McGloin, USAFR
Pip Moss
Tech. Sgt. Michael R. O'Halloran, USAF
Master Sgt. Clancey Pence, USAF
Tech. Sgt. Russ Pollanen, USAF
Capt. Steven Radtke, USAFR
Staff Sgt. Francis Repicky, USAF
Lt. Col. William J. Rolocut, USAFR
John Rossino, Lockheed Martin
Charles Rutledge
Sue Sapp
Lt. Col. Carl P. Scheidegg, USAF
Staff Sgt. Phillip Schmitter, USAF
Maj. Oscar Seara, USAF
Senior Airman Julianne Showalter, USAF
Lt. Col. Lamont Spencer, 164th AW
Reid Squier
Richard Titcomb
Senior Airman Tiffany Trojca, USAF

Military/Combat Photographs and Snapshots

If you have any photos of aircraft, armor, soldiers, or ships of any nation, particularly wartime snapshots, why not share them with us and help make Squadron/Signal's books all the more interesting and complete in the future? Any photograph sent to us will be copied and returned. Electronic images are preferred. The donor will be fully credited for any photos used. Please send them to:

Squadron/Signal Publications
1115 Crowley Drive
Carrollton, TX 75006-1312 U.S.A.
www.SquadronSignalPublications.com

About the In Action® Series

In Action® books, despite the title of the genre, are books that trace the development of a single type of aircraft, armored vehicle, or ship from prototype to the final production variant. Experimental or "one-off" variants can also be included. Our first *In Action*® book was printed in 1971.

(Title Page) An air-to-air left side view of the first camouflaged C-5 Galaxy aircraft. (Staff Sgt. W. W. Thompson III / USAF)

(Back Cover, Top) C-5A AF68-0222, "Triple Deuce," in original aircraft glossy gray/white markings while serving with the 436th AW at Dover AFB, but before application of the "Lead the Fleet" football marking.

(Back Cover, Bottom) C-5A in war paint. The "European 1" pattern was applied to almost all C-5s from the mid-1980s through the early 1990s. Though unattractive, it reduced the visual signature of the Galaxy.

C-5A maintenance is under way on AF68-0222 "Triple Deuce," Dover AFB, circa 1972. The airplane is on jacks and the nose landing gear has been retracted. The crew entry door is open, but the ladder is not fully extended. When Lockheed was hopeful of producing a commercial cargo version of the C-5, it was advertised as being able to transport 80 Volkswagen Beetles at one time. (Air Force via Mike Leister)

The Aluminum Overcast

The Lockheed C-5 Galaxy first appeared in March, 1968. It has carried many nicknames through the years: 'Fat Albert,' 'Big MAC,' 'White Elephant,' and 'FRED.' It is operated by only one service, the U.S. Air Force.

The C-5 Galaxy was built at Air Force Plant No. 6 in Marietta, Georgia. The contractor was known as Lockheed Aircraft (Georgia Division) when the C-5 program started, and became the Lockheed-Georgia Company soon after that. Before the final C-5 flew off, it changed to Lockheed Aeronautical Systems Company, Georgia Division, and later Lockheed Martin. The company is most commonly known simply as "Lockheed."

Two major versions of the C-5 were built: the C-5A and the C-5B. C-5A output consisted of 81 aircraft, between 1965 and 1973. The C-5B program produced an additional 50 aircraft, between 1984 and 1989. In the late 1980s, two C-5As were modified internally and redesignated C-5C. In 2006, the Air Force began accepting upgraded C-5s, redesignated the C-5M.

For many years the C-5 remained the largest aircraft in the world. Only the proliferation of jumbo jets has made the Galaxy size appear commonplace. Russia has produced two comparable aircraft. The first of these is the Antonov An-124 Condor, externally similar to the C-5 but with a conventional empennage instead of a T-tail. The An-124 is not as long as the C-5, nor as tall, nor does it carry as heavy a payload. It also lacks the range of the C-5. Its wingspan, however, is six feet longer than the C-5, allowing it to claim a "world's largest" title. When the Antonov first appeared, many called it "the C-5ski."

The Galaxy is a high-wing cargo aircraft, built primarily of aluminum, of semi-monocoque construction. It can carry a cargo of over 250,000 pounds for 5,000 miles, unrefueled (and significantly longer with in-flight refueling). The C-5 has a Fowler flap system and a series of spoilers usable in flight or on the ground.

The C-5A and C-5B came off the assembly line with GE TF-39 first-generation high bypass turbofans, each producing 41,100 pounds of thrust. The upgraded C-5M uses F138-GE-100 turbofans (derived from the commercial GE CF6-80-C2, which was ironically derived from the TF-39).

The C-5 can kneel on its landing gear, lowering the height of the cargo floor to a standard truckbed height. C-5As came with a crosswind landing system, but rarely used it. Lockheed built the C-5B without the crosswind capability and the Air Force later took the maintenance-intensive system off the C-5A. The landing gear permits operation from an unprepared surface. C-5s have successfully operated in up to 14 inches of snow, and in mud and soft earth, although landings in mud are considered highly unusual.

Minimum crew for a C-5 is four: pilot, co-pilot, flight engineer, and scanner. Loadmaster and crew associated with cargo add additional personnel. The C-5 can carry a relief crew of seven, an additional eight persons in the courier compartment in the area aft of the flight deck, and (except for the C-5C) 75 passengers in airliner-type seats in a troop compartment aft of the wing. A cargo compartment palletized troop seat arrangement allows 270 additional passengers, although C-5s rarely fly in this configuration. The C-5A, B, and M have three galleys: two aft in the troop compartment and one forward near the courier compartment (the C-5C has only the forward galley). The C-5 also has two bunkrooms for crew rest just aft of the flight deck. Each bunkroom sleeps three.

The cargo compartment is accessible through either forward or aft cargo loading doors, permitting drive-on/drive-off loading. The cargo compartment floor is 121 feet

The first C-5A (Lockheed Martin serial 0001, AF tail number AF66-8303) rolls out at the east side of Lockheed's L-10 building in Marietta, Georgia, on 2 March 1968. President Lyndon Johnson, the Secretary of Defense, and Secretary of the Air Force attended the ceremony. According to legend, on viewing the interior of the aircraft LBJ remarked "You could sure carry a lot of hay in this thing." Indeed, almost 20 years later the C-5 did fly hay to relieve drought-stricken farmers in the southwestern U.S. (Lockheed Martin)

Lockheed C-5A Galaxy

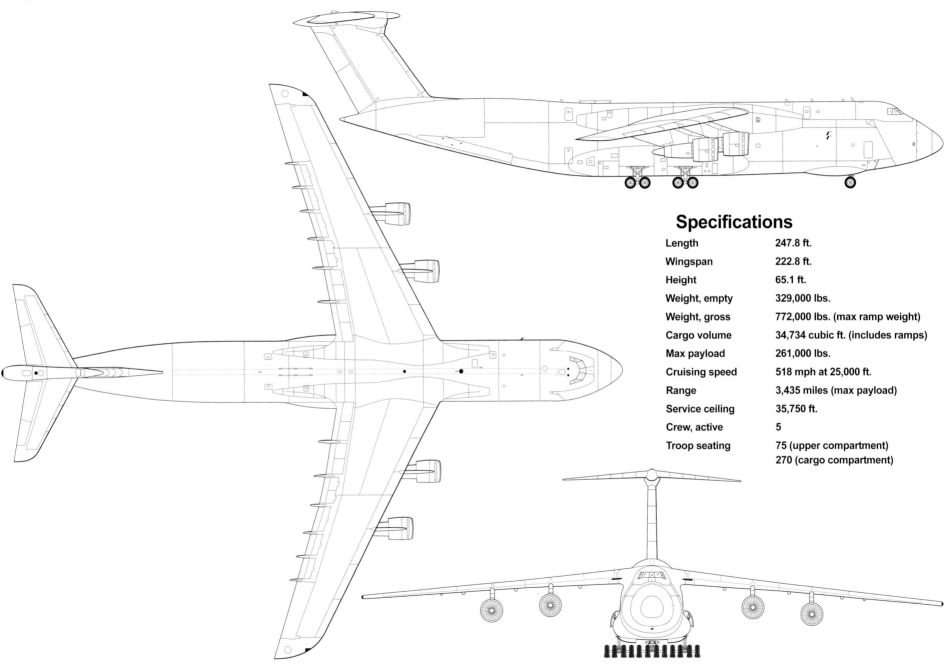

Specifications

Length	247.8 ft.
Wingspan	222.8 ft.
Height	65.1 ft.
Weight, empty	329,000 lbs.
Weight, gross	772,000 lbs. (max ramp weight)
Cargo volume	34,734 cubic ft. (includes ramps)
Max payload	261,000 lbs.
Cruising speed	518 mph at 25,000 ft.
Range	3,435 miles (max payload)
Service ceiling	35,750 ft.
Crew, active	5
Troop seating	75 (upper compartment)
	270 (cargo compartment)

June 1970, the first operational C-5A arrives at Charleston (SC) AFB (all Charleston airplanes were later transferred to other bases). The C-5A landed amidst a fanfare of publicity, tarnished slightly when one of the tires departed the airplane and went bouncing down the runway (note the arrow pointing to the stray wheel). Congressman Mendel Rivers (a supporter of the C-5) shrugged it off to reporters, noting that the C-5 still had 27 tires left. The incident, however, was almost inevitably brought up by critics. (Lockheed Martin)

Triple Deuce, AF68-0222, flies over Delaware Bay, apparently with a prototype composite leading edge on the starboard wing. This was not installed as a fleet-wide modification. The "football" applied to Lead the Fleet aircraft appears on the starboard and port sides, visible here ahead and slightly below the US AIR FORCE marking. (Lockheed Martin)

C-5A AF68-0222 "Triple Deuce" now flies with the 439th Airlift Wing, USAFR, Westover ARB, Massachusetts. In 1992, this airplane sorely needed a new paint job. Minor peeling areas in the nose had been touched up with a lighter shade of green. MAC references had been painted out, but due to fading, the paint color did not match. (Rick Lippincott)

6

long (about one foot longer than the Wright brothers' first flight). Usable cargo space is 144 feet long, because the aft ramp also supports weight. The fully-pressurized cargo compartment is 13.5 feet high, and 19 feet wide: a total volume of 34,734 cubic feet.

The C-5 is equipped to airdrop materiel or troops, although the Air Force normally does not use this feature. Due to its sheer size, an airdrop of troops or standard materiel from a C-5 would spread out over an unacceptably large area. The aircraft's size would also make it vulnerable to ground fire.

The C-5 contains an inertial navigation system and an on-board automated diagnostic system, known as "MADAR" (Malfunction Analysis, Detection, and Recording, rhymes with "radar"). Communications equipment includes VHF and UHF "secure voice" systems, as well as internal intercom and public address systems.

The aircraft has lifted the heaviest payload in the world, and since the early 1970's consistently set records for heaviest load airdropped. There is no "typical" cargo for a C-5, but it is capable of carrying any of the following loads:

- One M1A2 Abrams tank (Two Abrams will fit into a C-5 cargo compartment, but one tank weighs slightly over 50 percent of the C-5's maximum cargo weight.);
- Two M60 Patton tanks, and support equipment;
- One M48 or M60 bridge launcher, four M998 HMMWV (or variants), two M170 ambulances, two UH-1D helicopters, two M54 (5 ton) trucks with trailers, two M37 (3/4 ton) trucks with trailers, 52 drivers, troops, and support personnel;
- One M60 tank, one 155mm self-propelled gun, and one M113 armored personnel carrier;
- Up to 350 persons plus their equipment;
- Six UH-60 Black Hawks;
- Six M2/M3 Bradley Infantry Fighting Vehicles,
- Up to 36 standard 463L cargo pallets;
- 24,844,746 ping-pong balls.

Flight of fancy? Lockheed briefly studied this design, along with concepts for a seaplane C-5 and an open-fuselage "flatbed." Concept models graced the halls of the Marietta plant long after the ideas were shelved. (Model by Tony D'Anjou, photo by Pip Moss)

The Beginning

In the early 1960s the Air Force's airlift fleet consisted of three models: The C-130 Hercules, the C-141 Starlifter, and the C-133. None met the Air Force needs for strategic airlift of outsize cargo. The C-130 was designed for tactical, not strategic airlift, and lacked long-range and heavy payload ability. The diameter of the C-141 cargo compartment was the same as a C-130, so it could not transport the military's outsize cargo. The Douglas C-133 carried all outsize cargo at the time, but this piston transport was nearly obsolete.

In April 1964, the Air Force issued a formal Request for Proposal (RFP) for a new heavy transport system, the CX-LHS. Lockheed Aircraft had been building transport aircraft since 1955 at the company's plant in Marietta, Georgia. It was only natural that Lockheed would respond to the RFP and bid for the contract.

On September 30th 1965, Lockheed was notified it had won the airframe competition. (GE had been the announced winner of the engine competition, about a month earlier.) The Air Force ordered 58 aircraft, with options that could bring the total to 115. Jubilant Lockheed officials immediately began talk of different versions of the aircraft, and a production run of hundreds. One Air Force publication at the time even spoke of the need for several hundred Galaxies.

Though it lost out to Lockheed, Boeing had presented a proposal that became the basis for the first commercial widebody transport, the B747. The C-5 and the 747 resemble each other in more than size. The 747's characteristic dorsal hump is an area on the C-5

Early Design Concept

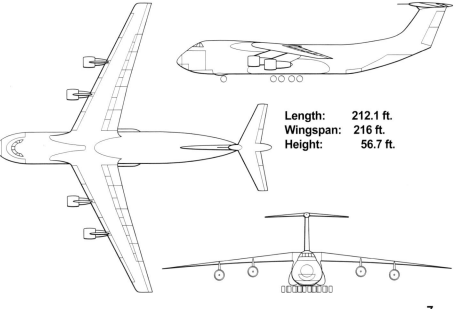

Length:	212.1 ft.
Wingspan:	216 ft.
Height:	56.7 ft.

In addition to the two C-5As in the foreground, there is a C-141 Starlifter in the background at the Travis AFB flight line in the mid 1980s. (Lockheed Martin)

A re-winged C-5A sits on the flight line in Marietta. To the right is Lockheed's L-10 building, the final assembly point for all C-5 aircraft. When it was built in the mid 1960s, the L-10 building was the largest cantilevered construction building in the world. Dimly visible in the background (just to the left of the cylindrical storage tank) is one of the C-5A engineering prototypes. This full-size fuselage continued to serve as a testbed for structural mod programs for many years after the C-5 production was complete. (Rick Lippincott)

occupied by relief crew and avionics facilities. Early C-5 designs (before the addition of the upper troop compartment) clearly show a dorsal hump similar to the 747 design.

Because Lockheed's "winning" design resulted in the production of only 131 airframes, while Boeing's "losing" design has resulted in the production of over 1,000 airframes, one may well wonder who really won the competition. The predictions of several hundred giants in the air came true, but most have come from Seattle, not Marietta.

The biggest challenge to the Lockheed team was weight control. By the end of 1966, any engineering change that would increase aircraft weight by as little as 1/4 pound required approval from a special weight-control team. Despite weight saving measures, when the first aircraft flew in the summer of 1968, estimated empty weight was about one ton over the guarantee. (As it happens, 2,000 pounds is the approximate weight of all exterior paint. "If we could only deliver a bare metal airframe, we'd make it" a Lockheed employee observed.)

Rollout of the first C-5A (Lockheed serial 0001, Air Force serial number 66-8303) was 2 March 1968. The first flight was on 30 June 1968 at the hands of test pilot Leo Sullivan. The C-5A soon began to set records. On 17 October 1969, it flew with a gross take off weight of 801,000 pounds. In December 1969, the Air Force got its first C-5A, delivered to the Military Airlift Command (MAC) training squadron at Altus AFB, Oklahoma.

Troubles loomed, however. The first Galaxy was not only the largest aircraft in the world, it was also the most expensive, at a then-whopping $60 million each (about 50% over the original estimates). Escalating costs eventually reduced C-5A production from the planned 115 aircraft to only 81. MAC received the last C-5A on 18 May 1973.

The year 1970 was in some ways the low point of the C-5's career. Congress was investigating the program, and there were calls for contract termination and grounding of all aircraft. In May, 67-0172 (Lockheed S/N 0011) was lost to an in-flight fire. There were no injuries, but there was major structural damage. The Air Force soon ordered the airframe hulk stripped for salvageable material. Engines, landing gear, and avionics came off first. The wings were removed, and Lockheed eventually took the empennage. The upper flight deck was sent to the museum at Travis Air Force Base, California. On 17 October 1970, an accident at Lockheed destroyed 66-8303. A spark from a mobile air conditioning unit ignited fumes during fuel tank purging, setting off three explosions, and killing one man on the flight line.

The next year, 1971, also had its problems. In late September, a taxiing C-5A at Altus AFB suffered a truss failure on engine No. 1. The engine and pylon flew off the aircraft, rose 200 feet, and then flopped onto the runway. There were no injuries or other damage, but the incident temporarily grounded the entire C-5 fleet and inspired the nickname "FRED," the last three letters of which stood for "Ridiculous Economic Disaster."

Flight testing went on as Lockheed tested full-scale (non-flying) engineering models. Wing flex tests done on a hydraulic stand first revealed a wing cracking problem.

Some of the engineering mock-ups survived long beyond the flight test era. A full-size engineering fuselage went across the runway to the Georgia Air National Guard facility at Dobbins Air Force Base (Marietta), where it is still used to train crews in C-5 cargo loading techniques.

A double row of 500-gallon rollable fuel tanks is moving onto the air transportable loading dock at Hunter Army Airfield in Georgia on 15 December 1972. A ground operator visible at lower left is controlling the dock movable sections at a console. (Lockheed Martin)

C-5A AF66-8306 is exposed to the elements on the flight line. Due to their size, C-5s are nearly always parked outside, and it is normal for the crew entry door to be left open in all weather conditions. (Lockheed Martin)

This M60 has driven across the perforated steel plating in the foreground, and is about to move up the cargo ramp into a C-5A. The mobile artillery piece is next in line for loading. (Lockheed Martin)

The C-5A AF85-0001 is in the foreground, while the C-5A AF68-0214 is the white airplane in the background in this photograph of the Dover flight line in the early 1990s. (Rick Lippincott)

C-5A AF68-0214 has just taken off. This is the first flight of 0214 after wing mod. MLG retraction is underway, and the bogies have already rotated so that the wheels are perpendicular to the direction of flight. (Lockheed Martin)

Nose gear doors slide outboard when open, as seen here on C-5A 69-0001. The "Air Mobility Command" visor marking (MAC became AMC in 1992) is typical for the late 1990s. (Karen Lippincott)

The right side of the nose landing gear door is seen here. This C-5 is partially kneeled. The forward jacking pad is visible to the right of the NLG doors. (Karen Lippincott)

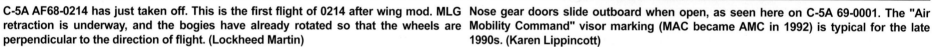

Nose Landing Gear

FWD

With 28 wheels, the C-5 requires no jacking for routine main landing gear maintenance such as this tire change on a C-5B. The airplane can kneel any one bogie or combination of bogies, facilitating landing gear maintenance. Dark fluid streaks on the forward main gear door testify to a recent hydraulic failure. (Karen Lippincott)

Main Landing Gear

When fully retracted, the main landing gear tucks up into the C-5's main landing gear bay - an open space along the centerline of the airplane. (Rick Lippincott)

Part of the landing gear and door actuation system is visible in this look into the main landing gear (MLG) bay of a C-5. The MLG pods were designed to provide as small a bulge as possible, to reduce drag. In order to accomplish this, the struts compress and rotate during the MLG retraction sequence. (Rick Lippincott)

The C-5 In Service

In June 1970, the first operational C-5 squadron was activated at Charleston AFB, South Carolina, and a C-5 landed for the first time at Kadena Air Force Base, on Okinawa. Former Tech Sgt. Joe DesRosiers was part of the ground crew: "We had C-141s coming in all the time. When this thing came in, it took forever on its final approach. It just hung in the air off the end of the runway, looking like Baby Huey up there.

"When it landed, and taxied over, I was supposed to direct the plane up to its spot on the ramp. He pulled up, and I went to the place where I usually stood for a C-141 landing. I looked up, and realized that I couldn't see the cockpit. I had to run up about another hundred feet before I could see the pilot.

"In those days, we had orders to change all the C-5's tires after every second or third flight. I had to call a guy out from the tire shop, and I told him he had a tire change to do. So he pulls up in his truck, and asks which tires we wanted changed. When I told him, he said 'You want all twenty-eight tires changed? I don't think we have that many spare tires on the whole island.'"

In April 1971, Dover AFB, Delaware, received its first C-5A. Two months later, the C-5 first appeared at the Paris Air Show, attracting crowds of viewers and remaining on exhibit during the entire air show.

The early days, though, saw recurring aircraft problems. Most involved the landing gear. There were jokes circulating about Fat Albert. For example:

Q: "What's the operational ceiling of a C-5A?"
A: "Field altitude plus jacks."

Q: "Three C-5As are on the flight line, and two are on jacks. What does this mean?"
A: "The base has only two sets of jacks."

In addition, the continuing problem of wing cracks limited payload and lifetime. The original design had assumed an aircraft lifetime of about 30,000 hours and a payload of about 250,000 pounds. The actual projected lifetime of the aircraft was only 7,500 hours, and the load weight was limited to 174,000 pounds (except for emergencies.) Despite these difficulties, the C-5A flew its first mission to Vietnam in August of 1970. As some thought the C-5 might make a good target for a Viet Cong attack, the aircraft was unloaded and back in the air less than an hour after its arrival.

As time went on, however, the C-5 began to play an increasing role in airlift to Southeast Asia, and MAC relaxed the aircraft restrictions. Flights from Norton AFB, California or Travis AFB to Tan Son Nhut became commonplace.

During a June 1970 mission, C-5A 68-0212 flew earth moving equipment to Cam Ranh Bay. In November of 1970, six C-5s off-loaded 171 tons of supplies in Vietnam, in one of the first uses of the air transportable loading dock, a collapsible platform that the C-5 can carry. Up to 60 tons of cargo would be off-loaded in 20 minutes. A flight in April 1971 carried three CH-47 helicopters into Saigon, and left with three battle-damaged choppers. In May 1972, C-5s spent 90 minutes in Da Nang delivering M41 tanks.

In the fall of 1972, there was a push to bring in as much materiel as possible before signing the peace treaty. Cargo included armor, supplies, helicopters, and F-5 fighters.

With the advances of the North Vietnamese army in 1975, the U.S. government drew up an evacuation plan code named "Frequent Wind," involving the evacuation of 8,000 Americans, and up to a million Vietnamese. C-5s brought food and military supplies to the increasingly desperate Saigon government.

AF69-0021 off-loads cargo in the early 1980s. This Dover-based aircraft carries a service marking just above the cheat line, over the crew entrance door. "MILITARY AIRLIFT COMMAND" has been added to the underside of the visor. (Lockheed Martin)

Cargo loading is underway at the aft end of a C-5. Kneeling a C-5 requires only a few minutes, but it does put stress on the airplane hydraulic system. Hydraulics failures while kneeling or unkneeling the airplane are common. (Lockheed Martin)

Operation Babylift

Tragically, the most widely publicized C-5 flight occurred on 4 April 1975, when C-5A 68-0218 (S/N 0021) crashed during "Operation Babylift." With North Vietnamese forces closing on Saigon, the U.S. was airlifting orphaned children and infants out of the combat zone. The aircraft had taken off with 328 people on board, reached an altitude of 23,000 feet, and was already over water when the rear cargo ramp broke loose. It blew out the back of the fuselage, cutting the hydraulic lines leading towards the T-tail. This left the flight crew with no control over the rudder or horizontal stabilizer surfaces. Aircraft commander Capt. Dennis "Bud" Traynor and copilot Capt. Tilford Harp used the only control method still available: asymmetric thrust of the engines. By boosting power on one wing, and cutting back on the other, they turned around and got back over land. They were within a few minutes of touchdown when it was just no longer possible to stay in the air. The C-5A broke up on impact in a rice paddy, killing most of the medical crew including Capt. Mary Klinker. Then-Lt. Regina Aune led the surviving members of the medical crew, and despite her own serious injuries repeatedly carried survivors through the rice paddy to nearby medevac helicopters, continuing until she collapsed. Due to the heroism of the medical team, there were 176 survivors of the crash. For their efforts, the flight crew was awarded the Air Force Cross. Capt. Klinker was the last female service member killed in Vietnam, and was posthumously awarded the Airman's Medal. For her actions that day, Lt. Aune became the first woman to receive the Cheney award. She retired as a Colonel in 2007.

M720 recovery vehicles and an M60 tank are off-loaded during the Vietnam war. The vehicles in the foreground did not come from the C-5 in the background. There is a vehicle, still tied down at the front of the C-5 cargo compartment. The aft cargo doors of the C-5 are not open. (Lockheed Martin)

M548 cargo transports are being loaded for shipment to Vietnam. Also visible is a Bell AH-1 attack helicopter. (Lockheed Martin)

A C-5A is ready to receive cargo at Cam Rahn Bay Air Base in Vietnam in 1970. (USAF)

13

Col. Regina Aune was the first woman to receive the Cheney award for actions following the crash of C-5A AF68-0218. Despite a broken foot, injured leg and a broken bone in her back, following the crash, then-Lt. Aune repeatedly waded through a rice paddy carrying the injured from the crash site to nearby medical helicopters until she collapsed from her injuries. She received the Cheney award, which is given for an act of valor, extreme fortitude, or self-sacrifice in a humanitarian interest, performed in connection with aircraft, but not necessarily of a military nature. (USAF)

Operation Nickel Grass

From virtually its first flight, and continuing through its entire production run, critics viewed the C-5A as a white elephant. An April 1973 editorial in *The Washington Post* slammed the aircraft as a "death trap" and "flying coffin." In October 1973, the C-5's image turned dramatically around.

The October War in the Mid East started with a surprise attack on Israeli-occupied territory, and within hours, the Israelis were in a tough situation, being driven back from land they had seized in 1967. They needed U.S. military equipment. The materiel had already been purchased, but it was in the wrong hemisphere.

Airlift was the answer. It would involve all of MAC's aircraft types and it was clearly time to put the C-5A to full use. On 13 October 1973, operation Nickel Grass was ordered. Less than 10 hours after the decision to assist Israel, the first C-5 was over the Atlantic Ocean. It arrived at Lod Airport, Israel, about 10:00 PM local time on the 14th, escorted by Israeli F-4s. In three-and-a-half hours, 193,916 lbs of cargo were off-loaded, and the aircraft returned to the U.S. C-141As also flew many supply missions to Israel, but the C-5As had a larger size and heavier payload, plus in-flight refueling ability. Quickly, an air bridge sprang up between east coast MAC bases and Lod. The Israelis got ammunition, trucks, helicopters, medical supplies, beans, and bullets.

When it was over, the C-5s had flown 145 sorties (about 25 per cent of all missions), transporting 21,600,000 pounds of cargo (about half the total cargo). In the process, they had flown 4,880 hours and used about 14.3 million gallons of jet fuel. Meanwhile, the Soviet Union began an airlift to its Arab allies. Due to the shorter ranges involved their task was simpler, but it was not as effective as the U.S. effort. The Soviets flew about 935 missions, but the cargo on each mission was smaller. Total Soviet airlift, requiring 40 days, amounted to 15,000 tons delivered over 1,700 miles. The total U.S. airlift (C-5 and C-141 combined) was more than 22,000 tons over 6,450 nautical miles in 33 days.

C-5 cargo during Nickel Grass included M60 and M48 tanks, CH-53 helicopters, and 175mm cannons weighing more than 28 tons each.

An M577 mobile command post is off-loaded from a C-5A. There is a protective plywood layer on the front ramp, a normal procedure when transporting tracked vehicles in a C-5. The M577 weighed 23,900 pounds, representing about half the weight a C-5A could carry during the years before the installation of the new wing. (Lockheed Martin)

Operation Just Cause

On 20 December 1989, U.S. military forces moved into Panama. The mission was to remove dictator General Manuel Noriega from power. Despite weeks of preparation by the American military, the invasion caught the Panamanian forces by surprise. MAC played a major role in the invasion with heavy C-5 use. For example, a few weeks before the invasion, AH-64 Apache attack helicopters came into Panama on C-5s.

During the first night of Just Cause, a dozen C-5s moved war material into Howard AFB in Panama. Air Reserve units, as well as regular MAC units, took part. This meant that the C-5s were flying into a combat area, and in some cases came under live fire.

Desert Storm, Desert Shield, and Provide Comfort

When Iraqi forces overran Kuwait on 2 August 1990, their bad luck began on the very first day. The 436th Military Airlift Wing at Dover AFB was in a previously scheduled Operational Readiness Inspection (ORI), and already alert. Within a short time, Dover transitioned from exercise to war footing.

Desert Shield was the largest airlift effort in history, bringing troops and material to the expected battle area. Most of the equipment used during Desert Shield and Desert Storm actually arrived via ships. The C-5 played a vital role, however, because of the need for speed. It took about 30 to 45 days for the ships to reach Saudi Arabia. Thus, during the first six weeks, almost all personnel and material brought into Saudi Arabia came by air. The first C-5 to fly a Desert Shield mission was a C-5B, on 7 August 1990. It was an 11-day mission, called "Bravo Flight", and involved over 80 hours of flying time. In order to reduce crew fatigue, several crews (including four pilots) went along on the mission.

The first leg of the mission was from Dover to Europe, where material was loaded onto the aircraft. The next leg, from Europe to the Persian Gulf, was called the "downrange" leg. Bravo Flight made four trips downrange on that first mission. They first touched down in Bahrain on 9 August at 6:40 AM Saudi time.

A relay system was established to keep aircraft in motion and allow for crew rest, but it still kept the people away from home. Captain Mike Fox, a C-5 pilot from the 436th, recalls that during the first month of Desert Shield he was in Dover for only 12 hours. During that month, he got no more than two or three hours sleep at any one time, a normal experience for the crews. The pilots didn't always know when they would be alerted for a mission, so sleep patterns changed to periods of activity broken by two-to-three hour naps. Crew rest periods were cut from 12 down to 10 hours for the first part of Desert Shield, but the 12-hour period was resumed by late autumn.

By the end of October, missions of up to 15 days had been flown, and 12- to 14-day missions were typical. Flight crews usually worked 26 to 28 hours at a stretch. Some "days" went as long as 35 hours, and 30-hour work periods were not unusual. Capt. Fox said that air traffic control was very busy; it was not unusual to fly over the Mediterranean and see 20 to 30 other aircraft in close proximity.

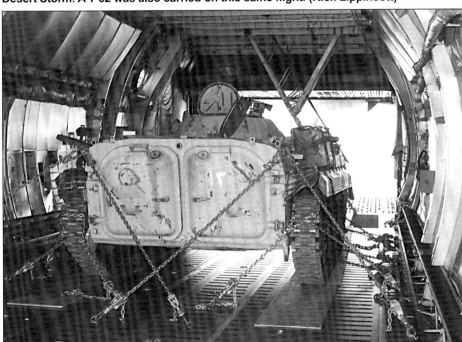

A captured Iraqi armored vehicle is chained down inside a Westover-based C-5A during Desert Storm. A T-62 was also carried on this same flight. (Rick Lippincott)

C-5B AF86-0023 is on the ground in Saudi Arabia, during Desert Shield. The first C-5 flights to Saudi Arabia took place on 7 August 1990. (USAF)

There are three phases to an airlift operation like Desert Shield.

Phase I is the mobilization of a base's own equipment, and deployment of mission support personnel. This phase takes two to three days. Loadmasters, maintenance, and command/control teams went to Saudi Arabia and other locations during this phase.

Phase II is the deployment of combat troops. The 1st Tactical Fighter Wing, 82nd Airborne, and 24th Mechanized Infantry Division flew to Saudi Arabia via C-5 airlift.

Phase III is the sustainment phase. In addition to new materiel, the aircraft are also bringing in equipment and supplies to maintain the readiness of those already deployed.

After about 30 to 45 days, sealift begins to take over. As soon as the ships start to arrive, the role of the C-5s changes to resupply, as well as unscheduled "essential" missions.

On one "essential" mission, C-5s helped maintain anti-Iraq unity. When Iraq fired SCUD missiles at Israeli targets, hoping Israel's retaliation would cause Arab states to withdraw from the U.S.-led coalition, the Israelis agreed to hold off retaliation in return for immediate protection by U.S. Patriot missiles. Within 24 hours, C-5Bs had Patriots and support crews in Israel. Dover AFB became the primary departure point for all C-5s off to Saudi Arabia, as well as the major point for aircraft repair. It is believed that all 126 C-5s passed through Dover at some time during Desert Shield and Desert Storm.

Later in the 1990s, the C-5s took part in other U.S. military operations around the globe, including as Restore Hope (Somalia), Uphold Democracy (Haiti), and Allied Force (Kosovo). The intensity of the Allied Force operations severely strained the C-5 fleet, particularly after the military budget cuts of the 1990s. Aircraft mission capable rates declined to 62 percent (75 percent is the Air Force standard).

A C-5B unloads during Desert Shield. The escape hatch located just behind the flight deck has been opened. This is a normal practice after landing. (Lockheed Martin)

Six C-5s are clearly visible in this view from the upper hatch of a C-5A during Desert Shield. On average, a C-5 landed in Saudi Arabia every 20 minutes during the opening weeks of Desert Shield. (Richard Titcomb)

USMC LAV-25s off-load in Saudi Arabia during Desert Shield. In September 1990, at least one Dover-based C-5 circumnavigated the globe on a Desert Shield mission. The crew picked up Marines in Hawaii, transported them to the gulf, and returned to the U.S. via Europe. (Lockheed Martin)

Troops board C-5A AF70-0452, bound for Saudi Arabia. Extra flight crews flew to Torrejon and Zaragoza in Spain, and Ramstein and Rhein-Main in Germany, to establish staging areas. One crew would bring a C-5 to the European base, and trade off to a stage crew. The stage crew would continue the mission. (Lockheed Martin)

C-5s load cargo for Desert Shield, in which nearly 30% of equipment was airlifted, and virtually 100% during the first six weeks of the buildup. (Lockheed Martin)

Operation Sapphire

In the fall of 1994, the United States bought 1,300 pounds of enriched uranium (enough for about 36 atomic bombs) from the former Soviet republic of Kazakhstan. Three C-5s from Dover AFB flew into Ust'-Kamenogorsk, Kazakhstan, carrying nuclear technicians, a mobile nuclear laboratory, and 500 foam-filled stainless steel drums. Six weeks later, two C-5s flew in, picked up the team and the drums, and flew nonstop back to Dover. The aircraft were C-5Bs, 86-0019 and 86-0020.

Enduring Freedom

Within days of the 9/11 attacks, military operations against the Taliban and al-Qa'idah in Afghanistan began with the laying down of an "air bridge" from the United States to Afghanistan. C-5s moved troops and material to staging bases, where they were transferred to C-17s for airlift into the theater. Unfortunately, it was not the C-5's shining moment. The budget cuts of the 1990s had crippled fleet reliability, and it showed. Early plans had assumed up to eight C-5s might be out for repairs at any point during the airlift, but at the worst of the breakdown period there were 22 broken C-5s on the ground. Airlift space had to be devoted to parts and spare engines for the Galaxies. Despite this, the C-5

Two crew chiefs move radioactive material onto a C-5 in Ust' Kamenogorsk, Kazakhstan, on 20 November 1994. In exchange for the fissile material, the C-5s flew in tons of badly needed humanitarian supplies such as warm weather clothing, sleeping bags, food supplies, and other items. (Tech. Sgt. Russ Pollanen / USAF)

17

At first glance, the C-5B appears to be swallowing a Boeing 747. During the first eight weeks of Desert Shield, C-5s were operating at two to three times their normal workload, flying about 1,100 missions. By early November, C-5s had accumulated roughly 40,000 flight hours in support of Desert Shield. (Richard Titcomb)

USAF Crews arrive in Manas, Kyrgyzstan, in support of Operation Enduring Freedom in December 2001. (Tech. Sgt. Efrain Gonzalez / USAF)

flew 4,425 missions (about 30 percent of all airlift missions) and delivered 210,000 tons (about 48 percent of all cargo).

Following the collapse of the Taliban government and retreat of al-Qaʻidah, the situation stabilized enough for C-5s to fly missions directly into Afghanistan.

In January 2002, a crew from Travis' 22nd Airlift Squadron transported a Navy Small Water Area Twin Hull (SWATH) boat from North Island to Afghanistan for "bottom mapping" of obstructions and objects underwater. The SWATH had been designed specifically to fit inside a C-5, but had only been loaded once before in testing. The 22nd AS crew successfully transported the SWATH, a smaller Zodiac boat, and a truck.

Operation Iraqi Freedom

The buildup prior to Iraqi Freedom relied heavily on airlift. C-5s flew about 6,200 sorties during the buildup, carrying over 330,000 tons total - just under a quarter of the missions, and about half the cargo. Following the fall of Saddam Hussein, the C-5s began flights directly into Baghdad International Airport (BIAP) in April 2003. The first C-5 flight into Balad Air Base took place in November 2003.

These missions were not without hazard, as insurgents more than once fired upon the big targets, and on at least one occasion scored a hit. Shortly after takeoff, C-5B 85-0010 took a missile strike to engine number four in January 2004. It underwent emergency repairs at BIAP, and then, in what is believed to be the first intentional three-engine takeoff in the C-5's operating history, was flown to another Persian Gulf location for more extensive repair. Final repairs took place at Warner-Robins Air Logistics Center (WR-ALC) in the US. The C-5B was back in service within 90 days.

The C-5 wasn't just reserved for the heavy freight, but also used to transport troops, a process that continued well past the fall of Baghdad. In early 2004, advance units of the Army's 1st Cavalry Division were flown in via C-5. Sgt. Carl Harz was one of many who rode a Galaxy into Baghdad; he described the ride as "comfortable," allowing time to relax and even sleep on the way. It was a sharp contrast to the bounce and crowded congestion of the C-130 that later took him out.

Disaster Relief

Some of the Air Mobility Command (AMC)'s most rewarding work is disaster relief.

In January 1973, C-5s rushed food, water, and medical supplies to earthquake victims in Managua, Nicaragua. A 1976 earthquake in Guatemala left thousands dead. C-5s flew in relief supplies, including a complete mobile telephone switching center to help reestablish communications.

The winter of 1978 saw some of the most severe weather ever to hit the northeastern United States. C-5As flew snow removal equipment into cities from Boston to Buffalo.

In the summer of 1979, Hurricane David hit the Dominican Republic. C-5s brought in helicopters, which flew food and supplies to isolated areas.

In October 1989, the New York Air Guard's 105th Airlift Group airlifted over relief supplies to Puerto Rico and the Virgin Islands following Hurricane Hugo.

December 2004 Tsunami

Operation Unified Assistance was a response to the Indian Ocean tsunami of 26 December 2004. Missions were flown from the west coast to Bandaranaike, Sri Lanka; or Utapao, Thailand. Cargo included shelters, medical supplies, food, ground vehicles, generators, and helicopters. Air reserve and Air Guard C-5s alone transported over 1,300 tons of supplies in support of the relief efforts.

2005 Hurricane Relief Operations

The 2005 brought a brutal hurricane season, with Katrina and Rita inflicting massive damage on Gulf Coast areas. C-5s started contributing to relief before the storms even hit, evacuating hospital patients out of the path of the storms. Among other post-storm activities, C-5s from Westover were used to transport helicopters, rescue supplies, shelters, swift boat teams, command posts, and rescue personnel. Three Dover-based C-5s flew to Holloman AFB, NM and picked up Basic Expeditionary Airfield Resource (BEAR) kits, and transported them to New Orleans. BEAR kits were used to construct tent cities for those who lost homes in Katrina.

Pakistan Earthquake

Within 48 hours of the October 2005 earthquake in Pakistan, three C-5s departed from Hickam AFB, Hawaii, loaded with troops, support equipment, and CH-47 helicopters. AMC managed a full response to the earthquake while maintaining support of Iraqi Freedom, Enduring Freedom, as well as the Rita and Katrina hurricane relief efforts.

C-5A 69-0013 takes on fuel in Saudi Arabia. In the 12 months from August 1990 to August 1991, C-5s flew about 23 percent of the passengers and just under 41 percent of the cargo tonnage. These figures include missions for Operation Provide Comfort, the Kurdish relief effort. (Richard Titcomb)

After the storm was over, the troops came home in spring 1991. C-5 pilots said that Westover AFB always managed to have a warm reception for the incoming troops, no matter how late the hour nor how small the number. (Karen Lippincott)

Two damaged C-5As rest on the Altus AFB flight line after a tornado blew one C-5 into the other in May 1982. Both were repaired. On the left is AF70-0467, the last C-5A. (Staff Sgt. Phillip Schmitter / USAF)

19

The center control console on the flight deck of a C-5B appears as manufactured prior to the Avionics Modernization Program (AMP) upgrade. C-5A consoles are very similar to this configuration. Throttle quadrants for pilot and co-pilot are located on the forward end of the center console; aircraft trim controls are nearby. The large flat portion of the center console is mostly for communication and navigation system controls. The horizontal guard bar towards the bottom of the console is a foot rest. (Karen Lippincott)

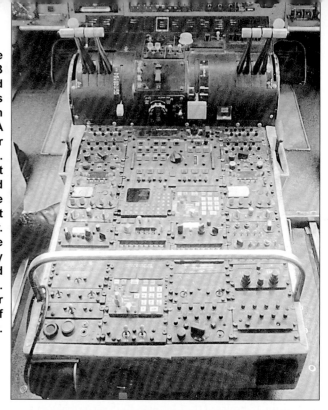

The upper portion of the flight engineer's control panel on C-5B AF84-0059 is identical to that on C-5A, C-5B, and C-5C airplanes, except for minor differences in the fuel quantity indicator faces on B model. AF84-0059 was lost in a crash at Dover AFB in April 2006. (Karen Lippincott)

C-5A/B/C Instrument Panel

The original, 1960s-vintage MADAR system is seen on a C-5A flight engineer's station. Instead of a CRT, the data were projected from film strips onto a flat ground-glass plate. To the right of the flight engineer's station are some of the many aircraft circuit breakers, whose panels are color-coded to aid in crew recognition. (Karen Lippincott)

An instructor pilot communicates to the aircraft commander during a checkout flight on a C-5B. The IP seat is permanently installed on the C-5 flight deck, and still allows plenty of room to get around. Women have been flying the left-hand seat on C-5s for years, and in fact missions with all-women crews take place with regularity. (Lockheed Martin)

This view of the flight engineer's station on a C-5B shows the MADAR II system installed on C-5Bs, and later retrofitted onto C-5As, This system was replaced during the Avionics Modernization Program in the early 21st century. MADAR monitors a series of aircraft functions and activity, and alerts the flight engineer if a problem develops in a critical aircraft system. MADAR allows the flight engineer to monitor less critical systems, and analyze a suspected problem. Then MADAR displays a numerical fault code that cross references to airplane technical manuals. The flight crew then calls forward to its destination to report these fault code numbers. This allows maintenance shops time to prepare in advance for the specific problem, and reduce aircraft down time. (Lockheed Martin)

21

Wing Modification

The roots of the C-5A wing problem go back to the design stage. Weight was a major headache in the C-5 development and was monitored closely by the Air Force and Lockheed. The Air Force ordered changes in the wing design, against Lockheed's advice. The Air Force design was the same size as Lockheed's, but used fewer structural members and substituted aluminum in areas that originally called for titanium. Pressed by negative media press and Congressional scrutiny, Lockheed caved in and made the lighter wing.

The C-5A had not even entered regular service when wing cracks began to appear on the engineering mock-ups. Immediately, a series of quick fixes were installed on the early models, and designed into the rest of the C-5 fleet. As time passed, it became clear that these measures would only be temporary. The cracks (hairline fractures detectable only by close inspection) did not appear on all C-5s, but they were appearing in predictable locations and were clearly a result of metal fatigue. The C-5s were placed under flight restrictions, and not allowed to operate at full load except in an emergency. (Operation Nickel Grass was one of those emergency exceptions, and it literally took years off the C-5A life expectancy.)

Finally, the Air Force acknowledged that the only solution was a total wing replacement. Lockheed won the contract. C-5A 68-0214 made its first flight with the new wing on 14 August 1980, and took part in a flight test program that lasted several months.

The wing replacement involved the removal of both wings, as well as the removal of the center wing box structure (a part of the fuselage). Removal and reinstallation of the center box was the most time consuming, requiring about six months. Ironically, the wing design that was installed during the mod was very close to the design proposed by Lockheed in 1965. It has since functioned on the C-5A and C-5B fleet without any hint of problems. The new wing restored the C-5A to full weight cargo capacity, and also restored the projected 30,000 hour lifetime. (In fact, the Air Force has enough confidence in the new wing that those 30,000 hours are measured from the time of the wing mod program. This effectively made the rewinged C-5As zero-time aircraft.)

Color Weather Radar

The C-5A was designed with an enormous Norden Multi-Mode radar. It was capable of many tasks, including contour mapping, terrain following/avoidance, radar approaches, and station keeping. But only the weather, ground mapping, and rendezvous beacon modes were used with any regularity. The 1960s technology radar also was a high maintenance item. The first Bendix AN/APS-133 color weather radar system was installed at San Antonio Air Logistics Command (SA-ALC) in the autumn of 1983, and the modification program continued at about the same time as the wing modification. The AN/APS-133 was considerably smaller than the Norden equipment, necessitating the installation of a Kevlar visor plug between the smaller radome and the front of the C-5 visor. Combined, the new radome and plug are the same shape and dimensions as the original radome. The AN/APS-133 was also installed as new equipment on the C-5B.

The first "production" wing-mod aircraft makes its first flight. AF67-0173 arrived at Lockheed on January 28, 1982 and was returned to the Air Force (ahead of schedule) on February 24, 1983. Once the program was in full swing, a C-5A would typically spend eight months at Marietta for the wing mod process. By the time of this photo, the Air Force had decided to camouflage the C-5A fleet. The new wing box structure was installed with the European I colors (both upper and lower surfaces). With the new wing installed, all payload weight restrictions were removed from the C-5A. The improved wing is expected to last about 30,000 flight hours, which equates to about 30 years of normal flying for a C-5. (Lockheed Martin)

Special Modifications

Most of the modifications done to the C-5 have been performed on the C-5A fleet, as they are the older aircraft. There were a series of configuration changes that made the A-model very similar to the B-model during the late 1980s and early 1990s. From the late 1990s and onward, major upgrade programs such as avionics modernization were applied to both aircraft to continue configuration commonality.

Radome installation is underway on a C-5B. A crane is used to lower the large radome and fuselage plug into place. A circular collar then holds it in place until it can be fastened to the visor structure. (Lockheed Martin)

SA-ALC, C-5As park outside the main depot. The upper left building was designed for B-36 bombers and was later converted for C-5s. There was space for the wings, but the C-5s had to tilt so that the T-tail would clear the door. (Tech. Sgt. Dan Allsup / USAF)

Countermeasures

The Air Force initiated the Pacer Snow program in the summer of 1990, with Lockheed installing an electronics and IR countermeasures system on two C-5s. The system included AN/ALE-40 flare dispensers and an AN/AAR-47 missile warning system. The systems were installed in both aircraft by the autumn of 1990 and flight testing took place at Eglin AFB, Florida, and Holloman AFB, New Mexico. Following successful tests, countermeasure systems were installed on all C-5B and one C-5A aircraft The systems were used frequently by crews arriving and departing from Baghdad International Airport during and after Operation Iraqi Freedom.

Rumors

In March 2006, *Aviation Week & Space Technology* published information regarding a purported two-stage-to-orbit (TSTO) classified program that had supposedly been developed by the US government in the late 1980s. The article stated that two highly modified C-5s were used in support of the TSTO program. *AW&ST* described these as "chipmunk cheek" C-5s with eight-foot fairings on either side of the forward end of the airplane (just aft of the visor). *AW&ST* noted that USAF documentation from the 1990s had admitted two C-5s were on "detachment" to NASA. The same article also claimed that there was a C-5 in CIA service with the letters "CL" painted in red on the horizontal stabilizer. Although the story is entertaining, there are a number of obvious problems (not the least of which would be the structural difficulty of making the "chipmunk cheek" modification). Use of a C-5 in a clandestine role would be unwise, owing to the large size and unique profile. Finally, the reference to the "detached" C-5s would appear to be an erroneous reference to the C-5C. If the TSTO program is real, then C-5 usage is likely, but not in the way described by the magazine.

A C-5A taxies on the Dover AFB flight line, circa 1968. All but one of the parked airplanes are C-5As. (Lockheed Martin)

This view of a C-5B visor shows part of the aircraft countermeasures installation. The four squares above "AIR MOBILITY COMMAND" are flare launchers, installed during an early 1990s. Also visible are the IR sensors, the small bumps on the left and right sides of the visor plug. The rectangular maintenance access hatch and small air scoop on the bottom of the visor plug predate the countermeasures modification. (Airman 1st Class Kristi Hare / USAF)

The C-5B

When the last C-5A rolled off the Marietta assembly line in 1973, Lockheed voices were already talking about producing more aircraft. Three events made this become a reality: the tooling, a foreign interest, and an airlift needs study.

In virtually all contracts, the U.S. Air Force retains ownership of the tooling used to produce aircraft. The Air Force can (and has) ordered the destruction of all aircraft tooling after contract completion. Once that happens, further construction of the aircraft type is virtually impossible. Following completion of the C-5A program, the C-5A tooling was not destroyed. Although some of the facts concerning this are hazy, the legend at Lockheed is that when the order to destroy the tooling was received, a mid-level manager recognized the short-sightedness and ignored it. Instead the tooling went to an out-of-the-way storage area in Marietta.

In 1974, the Shah of Iran expressed interest in purchasing C-5s. Lockheed actively pursued this sale, and for this reason preserved engineering and facilities. Although the Shah never signed any contracts, his interest kept the Galaxy's pulse beating for a little while.

The next factor leading to the C-5B was a 1980 Congressional study of U.S. military airlift needs, saying the Air Force should have the capacity to move 66 million ton-miles per day. At the time, the existing C-5A, C-141, and C-130 fleets could carry only about two-thirds that amount.

Lockheed approached the Air Force with an unsolicited offer of additional airlift capability, proposing to build fifty new C-5 transports for a solid, fixed price. What made this possible was the existence of a billion dollars worth of C-5A tools still in the Lockheed storage area. Lockheed's proposed new C-5 (originally designated "C-5N") would be very similar to the C-5A but included improvements such as a solid-state MADAR system, improved flight data recording systems, and a simplified landing gear actuation system. The little-used (and often broken) C-5A crosswind landing system was discarded in the proposal. All C-5B aircraft would carry the European I paint scheme in the same pattern as the C-5A.

The C-5B wing matched the modified C-5A wing. Access panels on the aircraft exterior were slightly redesigned for improved maintenance, and the C-5B included a pair of maintenance hatches on the belly. More mundane items made the list as well, such as a redesigned crew lavatory that reduces structural corrosion.

In contrast to the controversy surrounding the C-5A, the C-5B sailed through Congress without a whisper. Although the price per aircraft was about $120 million, it was far from the most expensive in the world. The C-5B cost compared favorably to similarly sized commercial aircraft, and it was about half the cost of the smaller C-17 that was on the drawing board.

The Air Force considered the C-5B against a proposal for Boeing 747's built to military configuration. For test purposes, a C-5A and a 747 at Dover AFB performed a comparative mission. Each was tasked to load five Cobra attack helicopters, deliver them to Andrews AFB, Maryland, and return empty to Dover. What was a routine loading

The first C-5B (AF83-1285) rolls out on 12 July 1985. Like the C-5A rollout 17 years earlier, this airplane was also rolled out from the L-10 building, but from the west side. The highest-ranking Washington official to attend this affair was Air Force Secretary Vern Orr. Local news media covered the event, and made sure to mention the $3,600 coffee maker located in the back of the airplane. At the time of rollout, Saudi Arabia and the United Kingdom were seriously discussing purchases of C-5Bs (British C-5s would have been equipped with Rolls-Royce RB-211 engines) Some at Lockheed viewed the purchase of 50 C-5Bs as simply the Air Force finally picking up the remainder of its original plan to buy 115 C-5s, with a few extra thrown in for attrition. By 2006, between retirements and attrition, the C-5 fleet in fact stood very close to that number. (Lockheed Martin)

operation on the C-5 was a nightmare on the 747, due to the height difference. The C-5 departed to Andrews AFB, unloaded the helicopters, and returned to Dover to find the 747 still there, its ground crew struggling to get the last Cobra on board. Once again, the C-5 had beaten the Boeing design.

The Air Force signed a fixed-price contract for 50 C-5Bs in December 1982. Lockheed promised to have the first aircraft in the hands of the Air Force in thirty-six months.

Rollout of the first C-5B, 83-1285, was 12 July 1985, and first flight was in September of that year. Delivery occurred right on schedule, 31 December 1985.

Flight testing of the C-5B was not nearly as extensive as on the C-5A. By this time, the Air Force had almost 20 years' experience flying the C-5, so the purpose of the flight testing was to confirm that the C-5B met the specifications and flew like its older sisters.

In 1986, Travis AFB and Dover AFB received their first C-5Bs. MAC very quickly began, as a former chief said, "Flying the hell out of the new airplanes." As the Air Force gained experience with the new systems, it decided to retrofit some C-5B systems on C-5As. Landing gear and avionics updates were quickly approved and installed.

The C-5B repeated the history of the C-5A, setting performance records throughout the world. In 1988, a C-5B landed on the ice pack in Antarctica, the heaviest aircraft ever to touch down on the ice. The next year a C-5B set a world record for payload dropped, 190,346 pounds and seventy-three paratroops at Pope AFB, North Carolina.

Delivery of the last C-5B took place in the spring of 1989. Although by then Lockheed had submitted another unsolicited offer for additional airplanes, the Air Force decided that 50 were enough.

The C-5B AF84-0060 in the foreground, the C-5B in the middle, and the re-winged C-5A behind, are seen during winter operations at Dover AFB. During the 1980s and into the early 1990s, the paint color mismatch permitted easy discernment between C-5A and C-5B models at distances well over one mile. (Lockheed Martin)

"The City of Dover," C-5B AF85-0001, prepares to take on a load of Marine Corps AH-1Js Cobras, at NAS Atlanta, in November 1990. In this mission three C-5s flew out 15 Cobras and 187 support troops of Marine Helicopter Attack Squadron 773. (Lockheed Martin)

The flight crew boards C-5B AF85-0002 at Travis AFB. This aircraft was the first C-5B assigned to Travis AFB, in 1986. (Lockheed Martin)

Palletized cargo is tied down at the rear of a C-5B. A C-5A is parked in the background. (Lockheed Martin)

The C-5C

NASA occasionally uses a truck/trailer system known as the "Space Container" to haul payloads intended for the shuttle. This container offers a specialized environment for shipping satellites to the Kennedy Space Center, and is similar in size and structure to the cargo bay of a shuttle.

The Space Container is slightly taller than a normal C-5 cargo compartment so the Air Force decided to convert two C-5As to the Space Container Modification (SCM, pronounced "scum") configuration. The aft upper troop compartment, including the floor, was removed on these aircraft. New structures were added to maintain airframe integrity. The rear pressure bulkhead was moved 66" aft, and was redesigned to a two-piece structure. Internally, the aft end of the cargo compartment looks very different; its ceiling is gone, and the replacement structure resembles an arched cathedral ceiling.

The only visible exterior change on the C-5C is the aft center cargo door. On SCM birds, this door was removed, and cut in half lengthwise. Each half hinges to the "petal" doors, so the entire door assembly folds out of the way. When closed, a seam runs the length of the SCM door, along the centerline of the aircraft. When the doors are open, they have an accordion-type fold instead of the conventional petal-type opening.

The SCMs were designated C-5C in the early 1990s. The aircraft are 68-0213 (S/N 0016) and 68-0216 (S/N 0019), and now operate out of Travis AFB. They carry no special markings to distinguish them from other aircraft.

In June 1997, a C-5C carried "Node 1" (the first US-manufactured component of the International Space Station) from NASA's Marshall Space Flight Center in Alabama to the Kennedy Space Center in Florida. The C-5C has also been used to carry a fully-assembled Atlas IIA rocket.

Node 1, the first US-made part of the International Space Station (ISS) is unloaded from a C-5C AF68-0216 at Kennedy Space Center's Shuttle Landing Facility on 23 June 1997. The Space Shuttle Endeavour launched Node 1 into orbit in 1998. It is a passageway connecting the living and working areas of the ISS. The accordion-fold rear cargo doors are the only external feature distinguishing a C-5C from a C-5A. (NASA KSC)

Aircraft commander Lt. Col. Bruce Sayre runs checklists prior to a flight of a C-5C at Travis Air Force Base. (Airman 1st Class Tiffany Low / USAF)

The C-5M

Efforts to improve aircraft are ongoing and constant. Reliability and maintainability have always been an issue with the C-5 fleet, and the first-generation high bypass engines were looking anemic when compared to similar commercial variants. In the early 1990s, Lockheed proposed an engine change program that would replace the TF-39s with GE's CF6 series; under this plan the modified aircraft would have been redesignated as C-5Ds. This idea died an early death, victim of the military budget cuts of the early 1990s.

By the late 1990s, even the C-5B avionics were aging. Also, the Air Force was facing increasing logistics costs driven by the C-5s unique engines. As a result, the Air Force decided on two modifications programs: the Avionics Modernization Program (AMP) and the Reliability Enhancement and Re-engine Program (RERP).

AMP would require a complete overhaul of the ship's avionics, communication, and flight deck. The old analog dials on the instrument panel would at last be replaced by flatscreen "glass" cockpit. New systems included the traffic collision avoidance system (TCAS), installation of full-authority digital engine controls (FADEC), and a ring-laser inertial navigation with GPS receiver. The AMP modifications also allowed the C-5 to function with the Air Force Global Air Traffic System.

For RERP, over 70 reliability points would be addressed on the aircraft. A new engine, the GE CF6-80, was selected and designated F138-GE-100.

The modifications were done by Lockheed Martin at AF Plant 6 in Marietta. Airplanes went through the upgrades in a two-phase process. The first phase was the AMP, followed by RERP. When the airplane emerged from RERP, the designation was change to C-5M (for "modernized"). The first C-5M (86-0013) was delivered to AMC for testing in June 2006, after flight test early deliveries went to Dover AFB. Program plans called for the upgrade of all C-5B aircraft, the two C-5C aircraft, and one C-5A. While the AMP modifications produced no external changes to the C-5, the new engines added at RERP had a big impact. The F-138-GE-100 engines are housed in new nacelles, much like those found on the USAF E-4B command post. The nacelles more fully encase the engines, with the bypass shroud extending further to the rear of the engine. The F-138s also use a sliding thrust reverser system that is dramatically different from the TF-39.

The first C-5M sits on display in front of building B-25 at Lockheed Martin's Marietta, Georgia, facility following a rollout ceremony, 16 May 2006. The airframe, AF86-0013, was originally manufactured as a C-5B. It is assigned to the 536th AW at Dover AFB. A red instrument probe extends from the radome. This is the first time a C-5 has carried an instrument probe since the C-5A test flight era (no such probe was ever used on the C-5B). The C-5M has larger-diameter F138 engines and shorter pylons. (Lockheed Martin)

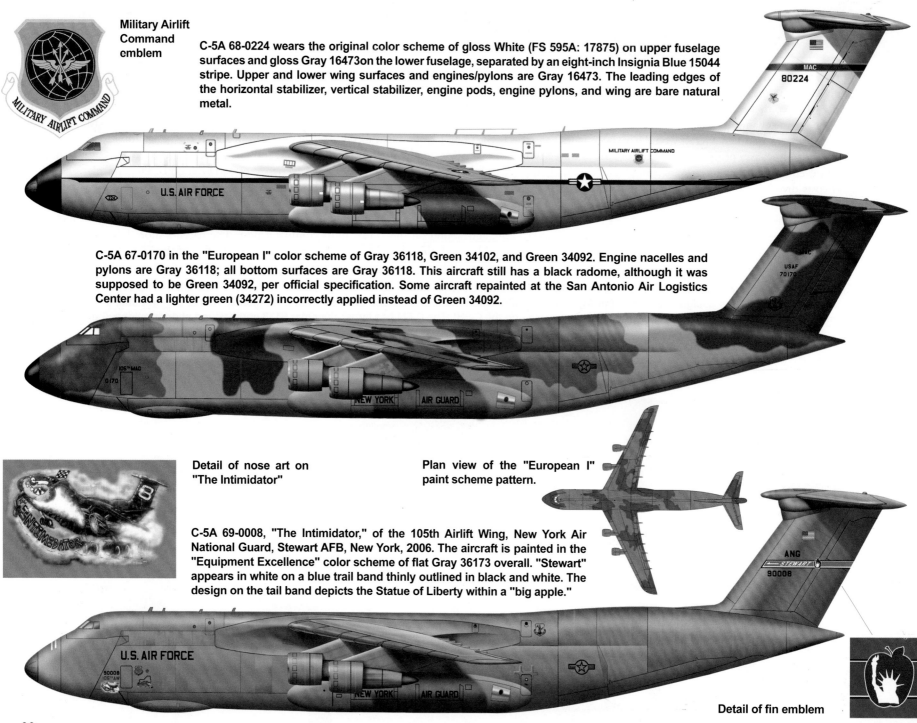

Military Airlift Command emblem

C-5A 68-0224 wears the original color scheme of gloss White (FS 595A: 17875) on upper fuselage surfaces and gloss Gray 16473on the lower fuselage, separated by an eight-inch Insignia Blue 15044 stripe. Upper and lower wing surfaces and engines/pylons are Gray 16473. The leading edges of the horizontal stabilizer, vertical stabilizer, engine pods, engine pylons, and wing are bare natural metal.

C-5A 67-0170 in the "European I" color scheme of Gray 36118, Green 34102, and Green 34092. Engine nacelles and pylons are Gray 36118; all bottom surfaces are Gray 36118. This aircraft still has a black radome, although it was supposed to be Green 34092, per official specification. Some aircraft repainted at the San Antonio Air Logistics Center had a lighter green (34272) incorrectly applied instead of Green 34092.

Detail of nose art on "The Intimidator"

Plan view of the "European I" paint scheme pattern.

C-5A 69-0008, "The Intimidator," of the 105th Airlift Wing, New York Air National Guard, Stewart AFB, New York, 2006. The aircraft is painted in the "Equipment Excellence" color scheme of flat Gray 36173 overall. "Stewart" appears in white on a blue trail band thinly outlined in black and white. The design on the tail band depicts the Statue of Liberty within a "big apple."

Detail of fin emblem

30

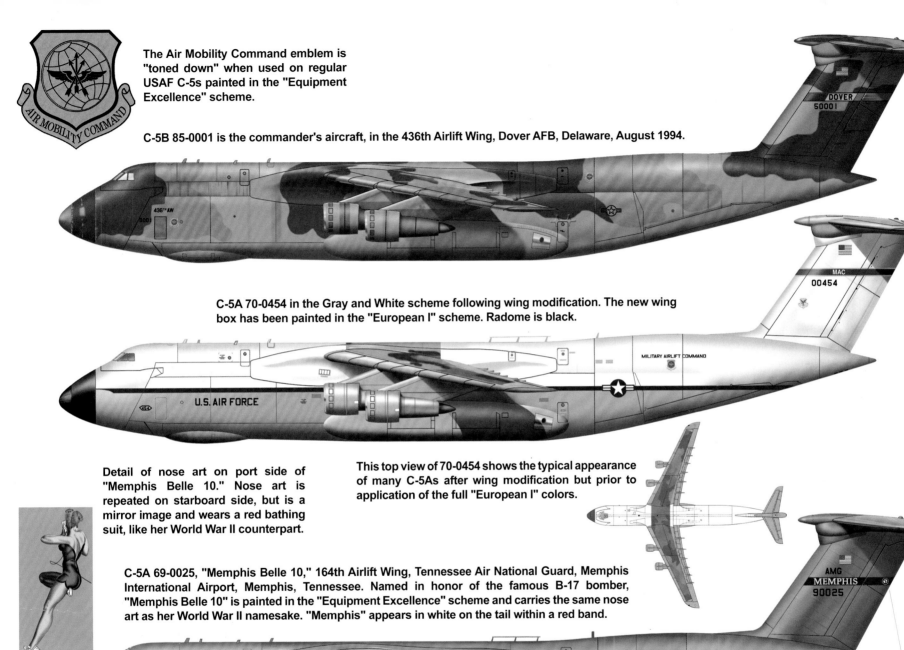

The Air Mobility Command emblem is "toned down" when used on regular USAF C-5s painted in the "Equipment Excellence" scheme.

C-5B 85-0001 is the commander's aircraft, in the 436th Airlift Wing, Dover AFB, Delaware, August 1994.

C-5A 70-0454 in the Gray and White scheme following wing modification. The new wing box has been painted in the "European I" scheme. Radome is black.

Detail of nose art on port side of "Memphis Belle 10." Nose art is repeated on starboard side, but is a mirror image and wears a red bathing suit, like her World War II counterpart.

This top view of 70-0454 shows the typical appearance of many C-5As after wing modification but prior to application of the full "European I" colors.

C-5A 69-0025, "Memphis Belle 10," 164th Airlift Wing, Tennessee Air National Guard, Memphis International Airport, Memphis, Tennessee. Named in honor of the famous B-17 bomber, "Memphis Belle 10" is painted in the "Equipment Excellence" scheme and carries the same nose art as her World War II namesake. "Memphis" appears in white on the tail within a red band.

Detail of Air National Guard insignia.

31

The C-5M makes its maiden flight from Dobbins Air Reserve Base, Georgia, on 19 June 2006. Upgrades to the venerable airlifter include new, more powerful engines; a modern cockpit with a digital, all-weather flight control system; a new communications suite; and enhanced navigation and safety equipment. (Lockheed Martin)

C-5M Number 1 takes off on its maiden flight from Dobbins ARB, Georgia, on 19 June 2006. In September 2009, a C-5M set 41 aeronautical records in one flight, including altitude with payload and time-to-climb. The C-5M carried over 176,000 lbs to 41,100 ft in 23 minutes 59 seconds. (Lockheed Martin)

Attendees at the roll-out ceremony for the modernized C-5M receive an orientation to the aircraft's modern, digital cockpit. The ceremony was held at the Lockheed Martin facility in Marietta, Georgia, on 17 May 2006. (Lockheed Martin)

C-5A/B/M Inboard Profile

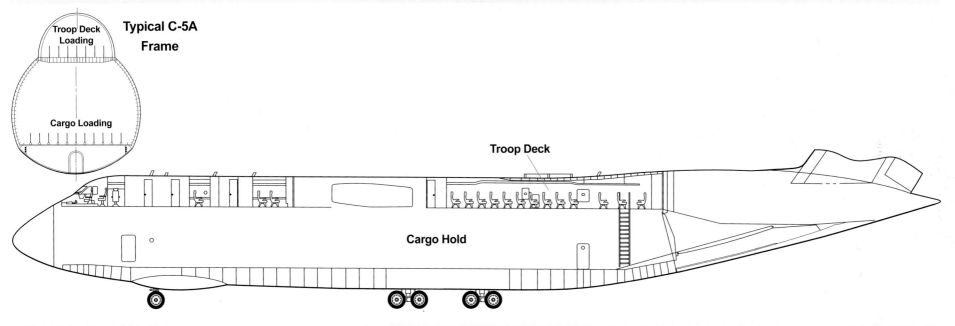

Typical C-5A Frame

Troop Deck Loading

Cargo Loading

Troop Deck

Cargo Hold

C-5C Inboard Profile

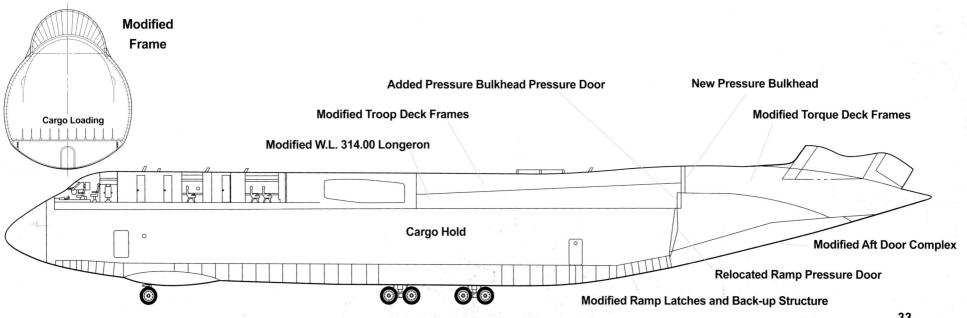

Modified Frame

Cargo Loading

Added Pressure Bulkhead Pressure Door

New Pressure Bulkhead

Modified Troop Deck Frames

Modified Torque Deck Frames

Modified W.L. 314.00 Longeron

Cargo Hold

Modified Aft Door Complex

Relocated Ramp Pressure Door

Modified Ramp Latches and Back-up Structure

33

A C-5B from the 439th Airlift Wing undergoes final preparations before a flight from Westover, on 8 September 2008. Westover Air Reserve Base is the nation's largest Air Reserve base. Originally built for bombers, Westover was home to the 8th Air Force and B-52s from 1955 to 1974. Following the 8th's move to Barksdale (Louisiana) Air Force Base in 1975, Westover's long runways and large hangers made it a natural home for another big airplane. C-5As began operating at Westover in 1985. The base transitioned to C-5Bs in 2007. (Karen Lippincott)

A C-5A passes the flight line at Westover. (Rick Lippincott)

Air transport specialists from the 332nd Expeditionary Logistics Readiness Squadron download cargo from a C-5 at Balad Air Base (Iraq), 7 January 2008. Loadmasters leave a path down the center, and walkways along the sides of the cargo compartment. With palletized cargo, the C-5 normally "bulks out" (fills the cargo compartment) long before reaching maximum payload weight. (U.S. Air Force photo/Staff Sgt. Joshua Garcia)

AMC and the C-5 in Peacetime

The most common peacetime missions, called "Channel Flights," are missions to transport supplies and personnel to bases in Europe. These missions are regularly scheduled, and carry supplies to Ramstein in Germany and to other US or NATO bases in Europe. The flights might also involve a support mission downrange going on to other locations. The island Kingdom of Bahrain in the Persian Gulf, for example, was a frequent destination during Desert Storm and Iraqi Freedom. The mission days can get long, a normal mission day is considered 16 hours. (An augmented mission carries an extra pilot, and the flying day will last 24 hours.)

A Channel Flight often starts late in the day; 8:00 p.m. Eastern time is a typical departure time from Dover AFB. The flight time to Germany is about seven and one-half hours, and therefore the flight will arrive around 10:00 AM local time. The crewmen get a minimum of 12 hours rest before receiving an alert for their next mission. Adjusting to jet lag is the biggest challenge. Under peacetime conditions, a pilot will average two Channel Flights and one training flight per month. That works out to a total of roughly 30 hours flying time.

A C-5A of the 433rd Airlift Wing taxies to the flight line in August 1988. (Rick Lippincott)

The 433rd Airlift Wing at (then) Kelly AFB operate these four C-5As in December 1988. The second airplane is AF70-0446, the "Phoenix II." In 1983, 0446 was severely damaged during an accident at Shemya AFB, Alaska. The airplane hit an embankment at the runway edge, snapping the keel and ripping the two aft MLG bogies from the mainframes (one landed in the snow, the other was punched upwards and came to rest inside the cargo compartment). Temporary repairs used timber and steel beams for a flight back to Lockheed, although 0446 still had so many holes it couldn't be pressurized. The airplane's nickname was inspired by the Jimmy Stewart movie *Flight of the Phoenix*, and appeared on the left side of the airplane. (Rick Lippincott)

AF70-0446, the Phoenix II, is back on duty with the 433rd AW in December 1988. Due to the repairs, the airplane structurally is now a hybrid of C-5A and C-5B systems. For example, it is the only C-5A with dual bilge hatches on the underbelly. Following the repair of 0446, the Air Force had the foresight to prepare several crash damage kits for future use. The kits were stockpiled at Lockheed Martin in Marietta. (Rick Lippincott)

Air National Guard and Air Reserve Units

As the C-5B entered service with the Air Force, transition of the C-5A to the Air Reserves and Air National Guard began. There has been Air Guard and Reserve activity at the C-5 bases almost since the aircraft first entered service. The mid 1980s, though, saw the emergence of C-5As being owned and operated exclusively by the weekend warriors.

Three C-5A bases were set up, two in the northeastern U.S. and one in Texas. Kelly AFB (San Antonio, Texas), became the first of the three, when the 433rd Airlift Wing took possession of its aircraft in December 1984. Following a 1990s BRAC, the 433rd was "transferred" to Lackland AFB when Kelly AFB was closed. The two bases were adjacent, so there was no physical movement of the airplanes or facilities.

In the summer of 1985, the New York Air National Guard got its first C-5As when the 105th Military Airlift Group at Stewart AFB, Stewart, New York transitioned from the Cessna O-2A Skymaster to the C-5. The crews, many of them airline employees, adjusted well to the change from the smallest Air Force aircraft to the largest.

The 439th Airlift Wing at Westover ARB, Massachusetts, had been operating Lockheed C-130s before taking over the Galaxy. In 2007, the 439th AW upgraded to newer C-5Bs transferred from Dover AFB, which began incorporating C-17 Globemaster IIIs.

There was a lag of over a decade before more C-5s were transferred to the guard and reserves, but in 2005 the 445th Airlift Wing at Wright-Patterson AFB, Dayton, Ohio, received C-5A 70-0457, the first of 11 C-5As. The 445th is an Air Reserve wing, and prior to getting the C-5s it had the last operational C-141s in the world.

The Tennessee Air National Guard's 164th Airlift Wing began receiving the first of nine C-5As at Memphis International Airport in 2005. One of these, C-5A 70-0449, was christened "Memphis Belle 10" in commemoration of the famous World War II B-17. The Belle sports the same classic artwork as her namesake on the visor, but six feet tall.

The 167th Airlift Wing, West Virginia Air National Guard, in Martinsburg, begin receiving C-5As in 2007. The wing was declared fully operational in April 2009.

Colors and Markings

There have been three primary paint schemes for the C-5. Only two apply to the C-5B and only one to the C-5M. A series of paint mismatches on the C-5A, as well as some variations caused by the major modification programs, has brought the actual total to about eight recognizable finishes, however.

The original scheme was glossy White (FS595A: 17815) on upper fuselage surfaces, and glossy Gray (FS595A: 16473) on lower fuselage and wing. It included a blue cheat line extending from the radome to the end of the rear cargo doors. This was similar to the pattern used on the C-141 fleet at that time. Although some call it the most attractive paint scheme applied to the aircraft, it was also the most visible. A C-5A painted like this could be seen miles beyond a point where a low visibility scheme would have faded into the haze.

There was very little variation in this scheme. The first aircraft, 66-8303, had the word "Galaxy" in blue script aft of the flight deck and above the cheat line. "Lead the Fleet" aircraft 68-0222 had an orange "football" painted aft of the crew entry door. Aircraft that flew missions to Vietnam sported campaign ribbons above the crew entry door. Aircraft 70-0446 carried the name "Phoenix II" during its repair effort and in service until it was repainted in the European I scheme.

In the early 1980's the Air Force decided it was time make the Galaxy look like a warbird and designed European I pattern using the two shades of green (FS595A: 34102 and 34092) and one gray (FS595A: 36118) common to the rest of the Air Force. Meanwhile, the wing modification was underway as was installation of the color weather radar so the new radome and Kevlar visor plug were matched to Green 34092. C-5A's began appearing still in gray and white, but with a green nose. Other aircraft were going to Lockheed for wing modification. Most new wings were installed painted in European I configuration (there were two exceptions). C-5As would fly for a time with a camouflaged wing box, and eventually go to SA-ALC for depot overhaul and the rest of the European I paint.

The two exceptions were 68-0214 and 68-0217. These aircraft received a glossy gray wing. They made occasional trips into the Soviet Union, and the Russians preferred that U.S. aircraft in their air space not be marked in war paint.

When the rest of the C-5s were at SA-ALC, the new European I paint was applied to most of the aircraft, but not to the already-camouflaged radome, visor nose plug, or wing box area. For reasons never explained, something went wrong at this point at the SA-ALC. Everywhere else in the Air Force, the European I paint scheme consisted of Gray 36118, Green FS34102, and Green 34092 green. When the newly-camouflaged C-5As rolled out at SA-ALC, the FS34092 color was missing. In its place was a much lighter shade, apparently Green 34272. There was a distinct color difference between the radome and the fuselage. An observer above the aircraft would also notice a mis-match on the Green 34092 portions of the wing. The sections installed at Lockheed had the right shade, the areas painted at SA-ALC were wrong.

The C-5A in the foreground, AF68-0224, has recently arrived at the Lockheed flight line, Georgia, in 1987, for her new wings. The engines have already been removed. It also arrived with a European I leading edge slat on the port outer wing. (Lockheed Martin)

It may be that everyone expected to see a big dark radome on the front of the C-5. It may be that everyone thought the paint had faded in the sun. Whatever the reason, seventy-four C-5A aircraft went to SA-ALC and came back with the wrong color. (In addition to the two gray and white birds, 68-0216 received its European I paint at Lockheed, during the SCM/C-5C conversion.) When the C-5B began delivery, the paint applied at Lockheed matched the proper specifications, and all the C-5Bs had a radome and plug that matched the fuselage paint. This made it is possible to distinguish between a C-5A and C-5B even when both were camouflaged. If a dark radome stood out like a sore thumb, it was a C-5A.

This situation continued up through the end of 1988, when some C-5As were returning to SA-ALC for their five year depot overhauls, and a second application of the European I paint. SA-ALC continued to apply the wrong colors. In the summer and fall of 1988, at least one C-5A even had brown paint in place of Green 34092 on portions of the fuselage. The fleet-wide color error was finally pointed out to SA-ALC officials, and C-5As started receiving proper camouflage starting in 1989.

There are also other minor marking variations. While at Lockheed, and before Air Force acceptance, the factory serial number appeared in large block numerals just aft of the canted bulkhead. Following aircraft delivery, the words "MILITARY AIRLIFT COMMAND" appeared on the underside of the visor, unit badges went on the fuselage near the crew entry door, and an American flag was applied to the empennage.

In 1991, the Air Force reorganized its command structure, and the Military Airlift command was replaced with the Air Mobility Command (AMC). Although the organization has a new name, AMC retained the old MAC badge, and these markings were left untouched on the aircraft.

"MILITARY AIRLIFT COMMAND" has been replaced with "AIR MOBILITY COMMAND" on active USAF aircraft. In the same location, Air Reserve/Air Guard C-5s have "AIR FORCE RESERVE," "AIR NATIONAL GUARD," or the unit number.

While there was little additional variation in regular AMC paint schemes, the Air Reserve/Air Guard units have applied some unique touches. C-5As based at Westover bore the legend "THE PATRIOT WING" in large block letters aft of the cockpit, on both sides of the aircraft. New York Air Guard aircraft carried "Empire State" in black script. New York aircraft also often bear the words "NEW YORK AIR GUARD" on the main landing gear doors.

While the European I scheme was useful in reducing C-5 visibility, it had two big drawbacks. One was maintenance. After any hydraulic leak on the aircraft, the spillage on the aircraft was nearly impossible to remove and made for a sad looking Galaxy. The other drawback was heat buildup. On a summer day a camouflaged C-5 might build up an internal temperature of more than 120 degrees. After Desert Shield, something had to be done.

By the early 1990s, routine wear was affecting the European 1 paint even on the C-5Bs, requiring touchup. Maintenance crews again began to apply color Green 34272 in defiance of the technical orders, causing a mottled appearance even on the C-5B. In 1991, the Air Force decided to repaint all of its transport aircraft in a single tone of flat Gray (FS595A: 36173). This is known as the "Equipment Excellence" scheme. The color is applied over the entire aircraft, including the radome and Kevlar plug. The first C-5 to get the new color was C-5A 70-0452, in mid-year. All aircraft received the Gray 36173 paint during scheduled depot maintenance, and the entire fleet had been repainted by 1997.

Thus there were six major variants of the C-5 paint scheme:
- C-5A original gray/white
- C-5A original gray/white with European 1 wing box and black radome
- C-5A original gray/white with European 1 wing box and European 1 radome
- C-5A original gray/white with gray wing box and European 1 radome
- Original gray/white with white and cheat line extended over visor plug (two C-5As only)
- C-5A European 1 paint mismatch
- C-5B European 1 "by the book"
- C-5A/B/C/M Equipment Excellence

AF69-0003 wears Equipment Excellence markings circa 1994. These airplanes now say "PATRIOT WING" in a red stripe on the right side of the vertical stabilizer, "WESTOVER" in a red stripe on the right side, and AFRC appears above the stripe. (Karen Lippincott)

There are four different radome marking configurations on these airplanes at the Stewart AFB flight line in July 1993. The words "Empire State" have also appeared in black letters on both sides of the fuselage. (Karen Lippincott)

Although the unit designation of C-5A AF69-0012 at Stewart AFB was changed to 105th AG (dropping "Military"), one of the two badges on the fuselage still says "MILITARY AIRLIFT COMMAND." "Empire State" is in scripted letters; the remaining badge is the 105 AG insignia. (The organization is now the 105th Airlift Wing.) (Karen Lippincott)

C-5A AF68-0214 still wears the gray and white scheme at Dover AFB in 1993, but by now the colors have been extended over the visor plug. The blue cheat line was neatly brought forward and tapered, as was done in the days of the Norden Multimode radar. (Karen Lippincott)

C-5A AF66-8306 in-flight, post-wing mod, and days after getting the first C-5 European I paint scheme (which also went over the black multi-mode radome on this airplane). This photo was often reproduced in the mid 1980s, with the tail number touched up and presented as a C-5B. The distinct darker shade of FS34092 in the wing box structure (and the tail number visible) plus the fact that the photo was taken in June 1983 (more than two years before the first C-5B rollout) proves that it is not. (Lockheed Martin)

C-5A AF67-0170 in EQUIPMENT EXCELLENCE markings, mid 1990s. "Empire State" is gone, but "NEW YORK AIR GUARD" remains on the MLG doors. (Karen Lippincott)

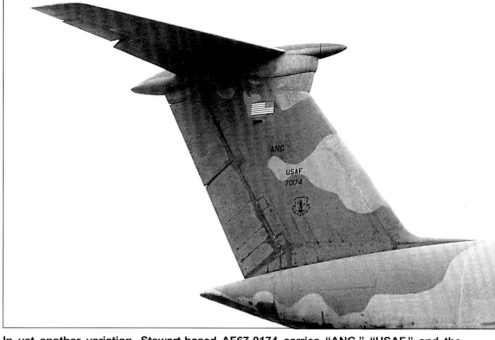

"ANG" has been replaced with "AMC" on New York Air Guard C-5A AF69-0008 with the appearance of the overall gray colors. (Karen Lippincott)

In yet another variation, Stewart-based AF67-0174 carries "ANG," "USAF," and the National Guard insignia on the tail. (Karen Lippincott)

Westover's airplanes gained a colorful tail flash (as seen in this empennage detail on 439th AW C-5B 86-0012) when the wing's aircraft came back with the all-gray "Equipment Excellence" markings. As a local feature, Westover's tail flash includes the symbol of the NE Patriots football team (used with team owners' permission). (Rick Lippincott)

This March 2003 shot captured a representative from what were then all of the "business" C-5 bases. Left to right: Dover (AF85-0003), Lackland (AF69-0004), Westover (AF67-0167), Stewart (AF68-0224), and Travis (AF69-0014) Only then-AETC's Altus AFB is not included. (Tech. Sgt Michael R. O`Halloran / USAF)

C-5A AF69-0025 comes in for a landing, painted in an early version of the Equipment Excellence markings. The vertical stabilizer says "MAC" below the flag. There are black anti-glare panels located in the area of the flight deck windows. (Lockheed Martin)

C-5A AF69-0001 of the 60th Airlift Wing is seen in the early 1990s. (Karen Lippincott)

This fully kneeled C-5A is in serious need of a new paint job. FS34272 has been applied as touch-up along the Kevlar plug aft of the radome. Eventually, on some C-5As, the FS34272 was extended across the plug and the radome. This variety of colors and variations on the European I scheme continued until the airplanes were repainted in the all-gray Equipment Excellence scheme. (Lockheed Martin)

40

The visor plug color matches the rest of the visor on this fully-kneeled Westover ARB C-5A. The radome is still FS34092. (Rick Lippincott)

Since the 9/11 terrorist attacks, many 105th AW C-5s have carried unique and individual markings of a patriotic nature. Many also carry small badges honoring NYC police and firemen lost in those attacks. New York Air National Guard C-5A 69-0009 shows the eagle, flag, and Liberty Bell over the Hudson River valley in August 2007. (Karen Lippincott)

Perhaps the sorriest-looking C-5A ever is AF67-0171, photographed at San Antonio Air Logistics Command in October 1988. The FS36118 has faded to a light gray on nearly all the upper surfaces of the airplane. The single exception seems to be the vertical stabilizer, where massive hydraulic leaks had stained the surface. (Rick Lippincott)

This C-5A at Stewart AFB has the same marking on both its sides in summer 1993. (Karen Lippincott)

There is a mis-match of colors on this C-5A on the flight line at Dover AFB in the early 1990s. The wing box FS34092 colors were applied at Lockheed during wing mod and are correct. The Air Force applied the incorrect FS34272 green shade during depot maintenance at SA-ALC. Seventy-four C-5As were incorrectly painted in this manner. (Four C-5As had been destroyed by the time the camouflage was applied, two C-5As retained gray/white schemes until going all gray in the 1990s, and C-5C AF68-0216 was painted correctly at the Lockheed plant.) (Rick Lippincott)

The first C-5A assigned to the 445th AW at WP-AFB is pictured here in October 2005. (USAF)

MAC markings have been deleted on this Westover-based C-5A photographed in 1991. Paint is mismatched at the squadron badge and number. Darker gray touch-up stands out against the faded FS36118 in the same area. By the late 1980s and early 1990s, the markings and colors of the C-5A fleet were suffering badly. C-5Bs, however, seemed to hold up better over the years. (Rick Lippincott)

Hydraulic leaks from the visor have discolored both the gray and green paint on this 433 MAW C-5A 66-8305, offloading cargo during Operation Desert Shield. The disadvantages of the European I camouflage were revealed in Saudi Arabia, where tremendous heat built up in the airplanes due to the dark paint. (USAF/SSgt. J. R. Ruark)

Strange Tonnage, Records, and Awards

The nature of "outsize cargo" dictates that what goes into a C-5 will often be unusual. There was an old joke that retired C-5s would be used at Davis-Monthan Air Force Base, Arizona, as a place to house the retired F-111s. It didn't work out that way, but the C-5 has flown with other airplanes as cargo. The Northrop F-5E Tiger II was one early example. Until the early 1970s Northrop completely assembled the F-5, and foreign sale aircraft were then flown to the customer country loaded eight-at-a-time into a Galaxy. The "first flight" of each Lockheed F-117A Stealth fighter took place in the cargo compartment of a C-5. At intervals of four to five weeks a C-5 would make a night landing at Burbank Airport and taxi up Lockheed's "Skunk Works." Behind cover, overnight two partially completed Nighthawks would be loaded onto the C-5. Before sunrise, the C-5 would pull away from the Lockheed building, take off, and fly east.

In his 1994 book *Skunk Works,* Ben Rich stated that in November 1977, the Have Blue Stealth prototype was airlifted by C-5 out of Burbank in the middle of the night.

The C-5 Galaxy has held or broken most of the world records for size and weight of cargo. Its records started with the beginning of the program, and continue today.

In December 1984, a re-winged C-5A set world payload records. It took off from Dobbins AFB and flew with a payload of 245,731 pounds. This aircraft also achieved the mark of the heaviest aircraft flown, with a weight of 920,836 lbs. To accomplish this, the C-5 took off with full cargo but a reduced fuel load. It was topped off in flight by KC-135 and KC-10 tankers to hit the maximum weight. The aircraft landed at a weight of 876,762 pounds; the highest recorded weight for an aircraft landing.

C-5 missions have resulted in multiple MacKay Trophy awards. The MacKay trophy was established in 1911 for the most meritorious flight of the year by Air Force persons or organizations. The C-5 won its first MacKay in 1977, when the 436th flew a 40-ton magnet from Chicago to Moscow. The flight originated at O'Hare airport, and with two mid-air refuelings, covered 5,100 miles in under 12 hours. This was the first time a Galaxy flew into Moscow. The magnet was used for research into superconducting materials.

The next MacKay Trophy came for a hazardous flight the following year. Military aid was airlifted into Zaire following an invasion by Angolan rebels. A C-5A (again from the 436th) airlifted 65 tons of equipment into the combat zone on a mission that ran from 20-23 May 1978. The aircraft operated under what were officially described as "hostile, combat" conditions, in an area that had no facilities for a large aircraft.

The 436th pulled a hat trick in April 1988, delivering 470 tons of outsized drilling and monitoring equipment from the US to Semipalatinsk, in the USSR. The equipment was used for a Joint Verification experiment at a remote Soviet nuclear test site. The aircrew completed the mission despite a lack of airfield or navigational aids and a need to fly around politically sensitive areas. This third win tied the 436th with the 43rd Bomb Wing (now the 43rd Airlift Wing, Pope AFB) for most Mackay Trophies.

In 1987 the U.S. aerobatic team flew to an international competition via C-5B. All of the team aircraft were transported intact inside the C-5, eliminating the need for reassembly at the competition site. This method of transport was very successful and has been used several times since the occasion seen in this photograph. The U.S. Aerobatic Foundation reimburses the USAF for the costs. (Lockheed Martin)

A satellite communications station is unloaded from AF68-0226, circa 1972. The aircraft carries a Vietnam service ribbon above the crew entry door. The airplane also shows signs of wear and tear, such as flaked paint in the white area above the cheat line. These are non-structural panels that cover hydraulic lines, and are subject to damage due to frequent removal. (Lockheed Martin)

Dover-based C-5A AF68-0217 loads Boeing B-17G "Shoo Shoo Baby" as cargo at Orly Airport, Paris, France, in 1978. Taken apart at the airport, the B-17 was reclaimed by the U.S. Air Force for display in the Air Force Museum. (Air Force via Mike Leister)

C-5A 68-0217 takes on a component of the European Space Agency's Spacelab in the early 1980s. By this time, "MILITARY AIRLIFT COMMAND" had been added to the visor, and the insignia forward of the crew entrance door had been removed. (Lockheed Martin)

This C-5A off-loads a Soviet-built tracked command-and-control vehicle in 1992. Although details are hazy, the vehicle apparently had been operated by the East German army and was donated to the U.S. following German unification. (Lockheed Martin)

A battle-damaged F-15 is loaded onto C-5A 70-0455 following the cease-fire in Desert Storm. (Richard Titcomb)

A Dover-based C-5B undergoes loading and unloading trials with the Army's prototype general purpose vehicle at Selfridge AFB in March 2005. As is common, the mission used a mixed crew of active-duty and reserve airmen. (Master Sgt. Clancey Pence / USAF)

A U.S. Navy twin-turbine MH-53E Sea Dragon is unloaded from a C-5A at NAS Sigonella (Sicily) 14 March 2003. The C-5s have transported nearly all versions of the H-53 in their service history, beginning with mobility tests conducted in 1971. The big helicopters require some disassembly to fit into a C-5 cargo compartment, unless transported by C-5C. (Petty Officer 2nd Class James K. McNeil / DOD)

NASA's X-31 Enhanced Fighter Maneuverability Technology Demonstrator Aircraft is secured inside the fuselage of AF68-0222. The C-5A was used to ferry the X-31 from Europe back to Edwards, after being flown in the Paris Air Show in June 1995. The X-31's right wing, (removed so the aircraft could fit inside the cargo compartment) is in the shipping container in the foreground. (NASA)

An Atlas 1 rocket used to launch the GOES-K advanced weather satellite is unloaded from Travis-based C-5B AF86-0024 at the Skid Strip, Cape Canaveral Air Station (CCAS) in February 1997. This is the final vehicle in the Atlas 1 series that began launches for NASA in 1962. The satellite was launched successfully in April 1997. (NASA)

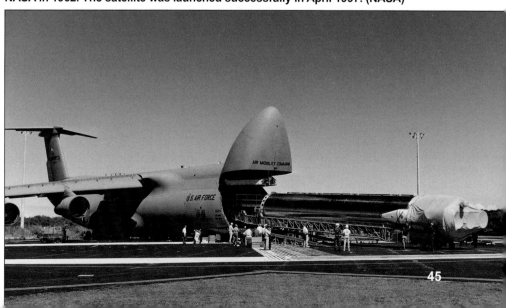

Cargo is being loaded in a C-5B. All C-5s carry an on-board cargo winch, stored in a well below the cargo deck level. Here the forward-most pallets have been brought on board, and the loadmaster is preparing to pull out the cargo winch for use in loading the remainder of the airplane. (Lockheed Martin)

Loadmasters are setting up the cargo roller system according to the tech manuals, preparing for a mission on a 436th AW C-5B in the summer of 1993. The rollers are strips, contained in the cargo compartment floor. Flat surfaces of the strips are up for transporting vehicles, roller sides are up for palletized cargo. (Karen Lippincott)

An M35 truck from the 82nd Airborne Division is driven into place in a C-5B in this 1988 photo. After parking, loadmasters tie-down the vehicles. The C-5 carries all necessary cargo loading and tie-down equipment on board, eliminating the need to position any ground support equipment in advance. (Lockheed Martin)

A loadmaster directs cargo loading operations at the aft end of a C-5. To facilitate loading, the aircrew can make the nose landing gear kneel while leaving the main landing gear at full height. This gives a slight downhill slope for cargo pallets brought through the rear cargo doors, and puts less stress on the aircraft hydraulic system. (Lockheed Martin)

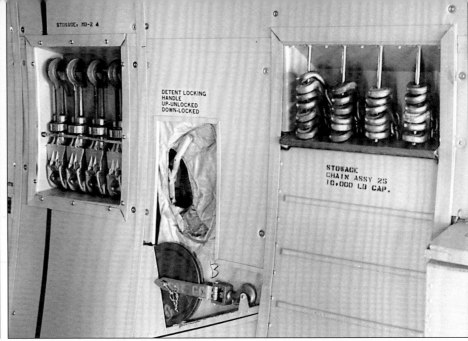

The roller strips, part of the cargo roller and retention system on a C-5, are normally stowed with the rollers down. They can be lifted out and flipped over in a few minutes. The guide rail system snaps up or down with no special tools. The rollers and guide rails, used with palletized cargo, extend the length of the cargo bay. (Karen Lippincott)

The visor is partially open on this C-5B cargo compartment. The stepladder near the forward ramp is standard equipment in the cargo compartment. (Karen Lippincott)

Tie-down hooks and chains are seen in the cargo compartment. (Karen Lippincott)

The C-5B cargo compartment interior includes these cargo loading controls. The two objects located near the top (in the padded insulation) are part of the airplane's fire detection equipment. C-5A/C/M layouts are identical, but A and C models were built using a rigid trim system in place of the padded insulation on the C-5B and C-5M. The forward crew entrance hatch is to the right in the photo. (Karen Lippincott)

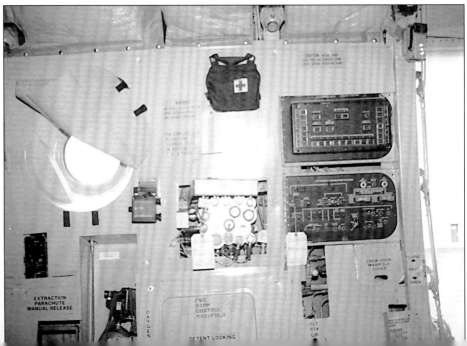

Both the ladder to the flight deck and the ladder to the rear troop compartment are lowered as a truck and trailer drive onto a fully-kneeled C-5A AF70-0459. Non-tracked vehicles generally do not require plywood protection on the cargo floor. Due to the C-5's straight-through loading, this truck was driven out the back of the aircraft when it reached its destination. (Lockheed Martin)

Westover ARB based AF69-0005 lowers the forward cargo ramp while on a mission at Hanscom AFB in July 1991. (Rick Lippincott)

The crew entrance ladder is an integral part of the door. When it is closed, the side will fold down to minimize intrusion into the cargo bay. This airplane is partially kneeled. (Karen Lippincott)

C-5B AF86-0015 is seen at Dover AFB in 1993. The dark stains just above the nose landing gear doors show that the airplane has had some hydraulic fluid leaks. The "knight's visor" upward-swinging forward door design was an engineering challenge, but was instrumental in the Lockheed contract win. USAF specification for the C-X required the ability to load/unload cargo from the front with all four engines running. Boeing used a simpler side-swinging mechanism, but it required shutdown of engine No. 3. That difference was enough to throw the win to Lockheed. (Karen Lippincott)

The upright cylinder appearing in the front of a C-5A cargo compartment is part of the forward loading ramp hydraulic system. Two small valves extend out from the cylinder, pointing towards the centerline of the aircraft. Loadmasters must use caution not to strike these valves while loading or unloading the airplane. On the C-5B, the valves were relocated to aim directly aft, reducing maintenance problems and adding four inches to the maximum width of drive-through cargo. The direction of these valves is a quick way to differentiate between a C-5A and C-5B in photos. (Rick Lippincott)

It's hard to find a hangar big enough for a C-5A, so the bases do the best they can. Hangars at Westover ARB, shown in August 1994, formerly accommodated B-52s, but the Stratofortress tail was only 48 feet high. A redesigned hangar door and movable scaffold system admit the C-5 empennage. (Rick Lippincott)

The single-point refueling panel is located on the port side of the C-5, between the MLG doors. (Lockheed Martin)

Two men in a bucket adjust an air conditioning hose leading into the C-5B flight deck at Lockheed. The camouflage colors of the European I paint scheme often caused the airplane's internal temperature to reach over 120 degrees, particularly in locations like Marietta, Georgia. This was hard on flight line crews, and hard on electronics. (Lockheed Martin)

Mechanics change an engine on C-5A 69-0002 at Ramstein AFB in May 2006. (USAF)

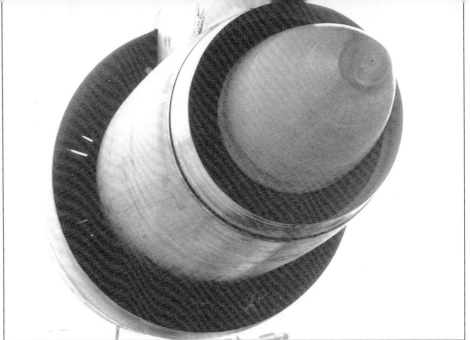

Tech. Sgt. James Gomez of the 8th EMXS works into the night removing the number four engine from a C-5B struck by a missile shortly after takeoff from BIAP in January 2004. (Staff Sgt. Suzanne M. Jenkins / USAF)

Bypass air flows around the cowl doors on the TF-39C engine; main flow air comes out from the area surrounding the "bullet." (Rick Lippincott)

Technicians are forced to work several feet off the ground doing outdoor engine maintenance on the TF-39. The systems' large size usually affords the mechanics room to reach in and perform work, however. A short, thin mechanic can actually squeeze into the engine pylon through the top to work on the fuel lines. (Lockheed Martin)

Dover AFB engine shop performs maintenance. The General Electric TF-39 provides 41,000 pounds of thrust, and was the world's first high-bypass jet engine. The TF-39 is thrust reversible, and can be reversed in flight. The engine has a bypass ratio of 8.5 to 1. High-bypass jet engines produce higher levels of thrust at lower fuel consumption than low-bypass engines. (Karen Lippincott)

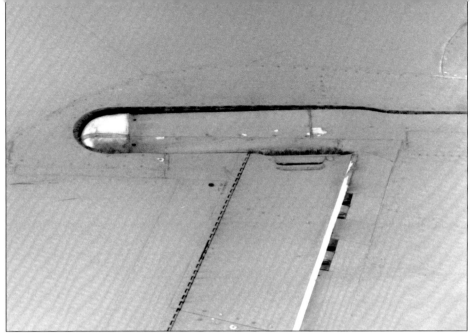

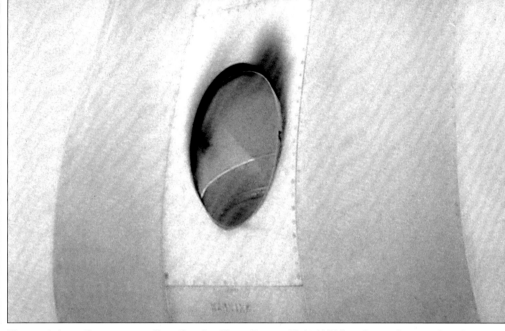

The silver-colored object is an aileron counterbalance made of depleted uranium, located near the wing tip of a C-5A. C-5Bs were built with tungsten counterbalance weights, and the tungsten units were applied to the C-5A fleet on an attrition basis. (Rick Lippincott)

The metal section surrounding the Auxiliary Power Unit (APU) exhaust is unpainted titanium. The C-5 carries two APUs, located at the rear of each MLG pod. (Rick Lippincott)

A C-5A horizontal stabilizer undergoes maintenance in Dover. Immediately aft of the open hatch is the Crash Data Position Indicator/Recorder (CDPIR), an airfoil with emergency beacon and flight data recorders designed to eject from a crash. A more reliable Emergency Locator Transmitter (ELT) has replaced the CDPIR. (Rick Lippincott)

There are angle-of-attack (AOA) sensors on the starboard side of a post-AMP C-5B, just aft of the AMC shield. There is an additional pair of AOA sensors on the port side. The L-shaped devices replace the original style blade-type. This difference is one of the few external indications of the AMP upgrade. (Rick Lippincott)

The visor lift mechanism is at the top of the forward fuselage. (Karen Lippincott)

There are four support pedestals on the cargo ramp at the front end of a C-5A. They support the ramp structure when lowered. Ramp extensions (commonly called "toes") unfold and lock into place when the ramp is lowered. (Rick Lippincott)

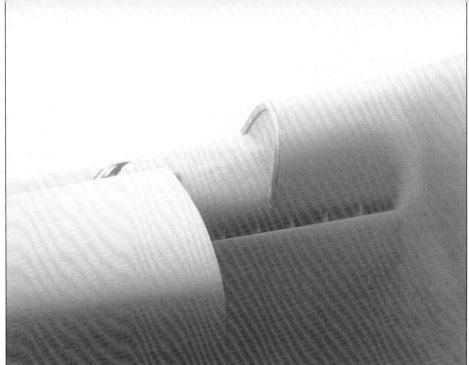

An extended leading edge slat and the air conditioning inlet are seen up close. (Rick Lippincott)

This extended leading edge slat is located on the inboard section of the port wing but is typical of all the slats. It is seen here from underneath.(Rick Lippincott)

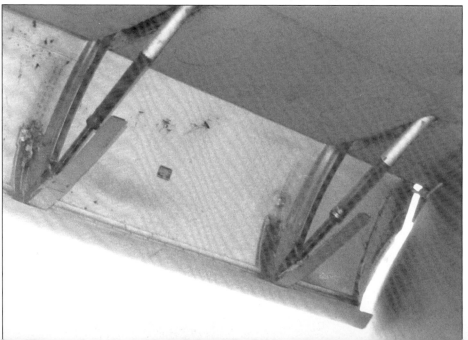

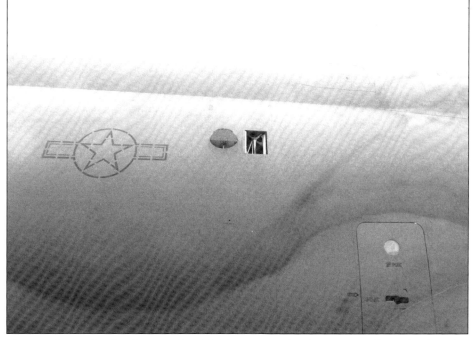

The vent located at fuselage station 1920 is seen on the C-5 exterior. (Rick Lippincott)

The two pitot-static tubes located on the port side of the airplane are visible in this view. Below and aft of these is the total air temperature probe. There are an additional two pitot-static tubes and another total air temperature probe in the corresponding locations on the starboard side of the airplane. (Rick Lippincott)

A C-5A kicks up some dirt in July 1991. Rough field tests in the late 1980s showed that the C-5 could routinely operate in dirt, mud, snow, and other less-than-ideal conditions, almost matching expectations for the C-17 but at lower cost. (Rick Lippincott)

AF69-0005 has just landed and the wing tip lights and landing lights are all still lit. (Rick Lippincott)

Attrition

As of 2009, a total of six C-5s had been written off. The first five accidents were with C-5As, the most recent crash was a C-5B.

* C-5A 66-8303, S/N 0001, was destroyed by fire at Lockheed in Marietta in October 1970 with one fatality.

* C-5A 67-0172, S/N 0011, was written off following ATM fire at Edwards Air Force Base in May 1970. There was no loss of life.

* C-5A 68-0218, S/N 0021, crashed outside Saigon in April 1975. Fatalities totaled 155, mostly children and infants.

* C-5A 68-0227, S/N 0030, was destroyed 27 September 1974, following an in-flight fire and emergency landing at Clinton, Oklahoma, municipal airport. There was no loss of life.

* C-5A 68-0228, S/N 0031, crashed 29 August 1990 during Operation Desert Shield. Shortly after takeoff from Ramstein AFB (Germany), a thrust reverser activated on the number-one engine, causing loss of control of the aircraft. There were fatalities. The aircraft belonged to the 60th MAW at Travis AFB, but was operated on that day by a crew from the 433rd AW.

* C-5B 85-0059, S/N 0083, crashed shortly after takeoff from Dover AFB on 3 April 2006. The crew reported difficulty shortly after takeoff, and was attempting a return to the base when the plane descended below the normal glide path, struck a utility pole, and crashed short of the runway. Seventeen persons were on board the airplane; all survived. Initially the crash was blamed on an in-flight thrust reverser activation, but an Accident Investigation Board determined that the pilots and flight engineers "did not properly configure, maneuver, and power the aircraft during approach and landing." A reserve crew from the 512th Airlift Wing was operating the C-5B.

In addition to the six listed above, 14 C-5As were retired starting in 2004. The tail numbers of the retired aircraft are: 66-8304 through 67-071 (Lockheed S/N 0002 through 0010), 67-0173 (S/N 0012, 67-0174 (S/N 0013), 69-0004 (S/N 0035), 70-0450 (S/N 0064), and 70-0458 (S/N 0072). There are no plans to bring any of these out of retirement to replace 85-0059.

Of the 14 C-5As selected for retirement, AF69-0004 was the first to stand down. It ended its days at WR-ALC. (Air Force photo by Sue Sapp)

The AF84-0059 essentially jackknifed on impact in April 2006. Crew chiefs were strapped into the seats visible in this photo, and were facing open air with feet dangling when the nose of the airplane came to a halt. (USAF)

Emergency responders are on the scene of the crash of C-5B 84-0059 at Dover Air Force Base, Delaware. An Air Force Accident Investigation Board blamed the accident on a series of pilot and crew mistakes. (Doug Curran / USAF)

C-5 Serial Numbers

Air Force Tail Number	Lockheed Production Number
C-5A	
AF66-8303 - AF66-8307	0001 - 0005
AF67-0167 - AF67-0174	0006 - 0013
AF68-0211 - AF68-0212	0014 - 0015
AF68-0214 - AF68-0215	0017 - 0018
AF68-0217 - AF68-0228	0020 - 0031
AF69-0001 - AF69-0027	0032 - 0058
AF70-0445 - AF70-0467	0059 - 0081
C-5B	
AF83-1285	0082
AF84-0059 - AF84-0062	0083 - 0086
AF85-0001 - AF85-0010	0087 - 0096
AF86-0011 - AF86-0026	0097 - 0112
AF87-0027 - AF87-0045	0113 - 0131
C-5C (C-5A SCM Program)	
AF68-0213	0016
AF68-0216	0019

"Big MAC" (the C-5B) and "Quarter Pounder" (the C-141B) fly in formation at low level. (USAF)

A C-5A is refueled by a KC-10. The C-5 airframe was actually proposed to the Air Force in a refueling version for the KC-X competition, this early proposal was the first use of the designation "C-5B." The Air Force elected to go with designs based on commercial widebody trijets. (Lockheed)

57

Training

The Air Education and Training Command (AETC) of the US Air Force ensures that pilots, flight crews, and ground crews are fully qualified to operate and maintain all aircraft and systems. Primary training for the C-5 has been carried out in two different locations. From 1968 through 2007, C-5 training was conducted at Altus AFB, Oklahoma. In July 2007, the responsibility for training was shifted to the 433rd AW at Lackland AFB. The C-5s operated at Altus were transferred to the West Virginia ANG, and the 433rd AW picked up the training role, using about half of its aircraft (the other half continue to conduct operational missions).

The 433rd provides initial and advanced flight qualification for AMC, ANG, and AFRC aircrews. Over 70 selectively manned aircrew instructors train and produce up to 500 aircrew members in nine different curricula for pilots, loadmasters, and engineers.

The 433rd AW also provides airlift support for peacetime, contingency, and humanitarian operations.

Crew chiefs with the 433rd AW Maintenance Squadron had to learn a few new tricks when their C-5A returned to Lackland with the new AMP avionics upgrades. The Alamo Wing was the first C-5 unit to get the upgrade for the A model. AMP upgrades replace analog avionics instruments with digital electronic equipment. The C-5 fleet has received continuous incremental avionics upgrades since it entered service, but AMP represents the third generation of avionics installed into the design. The C-5 avionics compartment configuration facilitates these changes (and maintenance), giving easy access to the systems. The C-5 has four avionics bays. Two bays are located in each of two compartments the size of walk-in closets. (Airman Brian McGloin / USAF)

A student pilot prepares for a training flight at the 433rd AW, Lackland AFB. The airplane has undergone the AMP instrumentation update. The 433rd AW must train crews in the use of the AMP aircraft as well as the "legacy" (pre-AMP) systems. (Rick Lippincott)

The loadmaster training system was built using components salvaged from a retired C-5A. It has fully-functional forward and aft ramps, allowing students to train on real-world hardware. (Rick Lippincott)

Tail flashes, like the 433rd AW Tail Flash on C-5A 70-0466, provide a splash of color and local pride to the C-5s, with the ANG and ARF designs showing the most individuality. Colors began creeping back into C-5 markings in the 1990s. (Rick Lippincott)

C-5A 69-0007 departs from the Lackland AFB runway at the start of a training mission. The buildings seen in the background were once part of the former SA-ALC. (Rick Lippincott)

A C-5 from the Air Force Reserve Command's 433rd Airlift Wing at a deployed location gets ready to depart on another mission in support of Operation Iraqi Freedom. (Capt. Jeremy Angel / USAF, 357th Airlift Squadron)

A UH-1Y Huey is winched into a C-5B at Travis AFB, 20 April 2009. Teams from the USAF, USMC, and contractors came together to determine how the new UH-1Y and AH-1Z Super Cobra helicopters best fit into the cargo bay of the C-5. (Lance Cheung / USAF)

The forward two landing gear bogies are gone, the rear bogies won't retract, and leaks in the fuselage prevent aircraft pressurization during the flight of 70-0446 from Alaska to Marietta, Georgia, after the 1983 crash. (Staff Sgt. Steven Colburn / USAF)

Damage to right landing gear area on the 70-0446 is visible shortly after landing in Marietta, Georgia. The forward main landing gear bogie was torn from the aircraft's mainframe. (USAF Photo by Staff Sgt. Steven Colburn)

C-5A 70-0446 is on the ground at Shemya, Alaska, shortly after the July 1983 crash. Due to the importance of operations from Shemya, salvage crews faced a tight deadline that amounted to: "You will move that airplane now, or we will move it off using bulldozers." The airplane was jacked and moved in tie, and prepped for the long flight back. (Keith Boughner)

C-5A 70-0446 is on the 443rd AW active flightline in August 2009. (Rick Lippincott)

Crew members on a C-5B from Dover AFB work with the 332nd Expeditionary Logistics Readiness Squadron at Balad Air Base, Iraq. They are loading a US Army Stryker Infantry Carrier Vehicle for transport back to the United States on 25 June 2008. (Senior Airman Julianne Showalter / USAF)

A Northrop F-5 Tiger II aircraft is being loaded aboard a C-5 Galaxy for shipment to Jordan in September 1981. (Garfield F. Jones / USAF)

Dover crews reconfigure a C-5B in Balad, Iraq, in preparation for a helicopter load in June 2007. (Senior Airman Tiffany Trojca / USAF)

A Dover-based C-5B meets a Kenyan Air Force F-5 at Moi International Airport in August 1994. Due to the economies of scale, from the 1970s forward, F-5 deliveries were made by loading the aircraft onto pallets and then shipping them to customers via C-5. (Senior Airman Andy Dunaway / USAF)

Circuit breaker panels are color-coded for faster system recognition at the flight engineer station on a post-AMP C-5B at Westover ARB. (Rick Lippincott)

Originally designed as a navigator's station, this cockpit position is now used as an ad-hoc business workstation on C-5s. (Rick Lippincott)

Flight crew relief seats appear in the foreground of this view towards the cockpit. Down the corridor, avionics bays are on the right, bunkrooms on the left. (Rick Lippincott)

Seating for 75 is standard on the upper troop deck, seen here from the rear. Passenger seats on C-5s face towards the rear. (Rick Lippincott)

The galley located aft on the upper troop deck contains the once-controversial coffee maker. The two round hatches on left lead to the "loft," an unused and unpressurized area near the vertical stabilizer. (Rick Lippincott)

The loft area is left empty for weight and balance purposes, and is not pressurized during flight. The loft area is larger than the cargo compartment of a C-130. A ladder leads up through vertical stabilizer to the access hatch at the top of the T-tail. (Rick Lippincott)

Tech. Sgt. Michael Vogt de-ices Westover C-5A 70-0449 before a flight in February 2005. New England storms that dump a foot or more of snow are not uncommon and complicate flight operations. (Tech. Sgt. Andrew Biscoe / USAF)

The C-5B is not as maneuverable as a fighter or attack aircraft and is not expected to be. In this photo, leading edge slats are fully extended. The small dark square extending outwards just below the port wing root is the air scoop for the airplane's air conditioning system. The scoop is fully extended in this photograph. (USAF)